Connective Career Crafting

Mastering the Art of Networking and Relationship Building for Professional Success

Written by
Morgan E. Blake

Independently published
2024

Copyright © 2024 by Morgan E. Blake

All rights reserved.

No part of this publication may be reproduced, distributed, or transmitted in any form or by any means, including photocopying, recording, or other electronic or mechanical methods, without the prior written permission of the publisher, except in the case of brief quotations embodied in critical reviews and certain other noncommercial uses permitted by copyright law.

For permission requests, write to the publisher, addressed "Attention: Permissions Coordinator," at the address below.

info@socialized.cloud

Published by Morgan E. Blake

Book Layout ©2024 Morgan E. Blake

Cover Design ©2024 Morgan E. Blake

ISBN: 9798325924217

First Printing, 2024

Introduction

The Vital Role of Networking in Today's Job Market

In a world where opportunities often hinge on the strength of one's professional connections, understanding the **vital role of networking** in today's job market is not merely an advantage—it's a necessity. This chapter lays the groundwork for a profound exploration into how and why networking forms the backbone of career success in the modern economic landscape.

At its core, networking is about **building relationships** that are mutually beneficial. It's a strategic activity that involves connecting with others to exchange information, support, and resources. The importance of networking cannot be overstated, especially in a dynamic job market that is increasingly characterized by rapid technological advancements and shifting economic conditions. The ability to adapt and connect with key players in various industries can set the stage for incredible opportunities that might not be accessible through traditional job seeking methods.

The digital age has significantly transformed the way professionals connect with each other. **Online**

platforms such as LinkedIn, Twitter, and industry-specific forums have become essential tools for networking, allowing for the cultivation of professional relationships beyond geographical boundaries. These platforms provide a venue for sharing expertise, gaining industry insights, and identifying potential career opportunities. They underscore the modern ethos of networking: being visible and valuable in a virtual world where the next big opportunity might just be a click away.

Furthermore, effective networking is crucial not only for job seekers but also for those seeking to climb the corporate ladder or pivot to new career paths. It opens doors to mentorship, partnerships, and collaborations that can propel a career forward in unexpected and fruitful ways. The exchange of ideas and resources among network contacts fosters innovation and professional growth, making networking a powerful tool for career development.

Networking also plays a critical role in understanding and navigating the **hidden job market**—the vast majority of job vacancies that are never advertised but instead filled through word of mouth or internal referrals. By building a robust network, professionals gain access to this hidden market, often learning about opportunities before they are publicly known. The adage "It's not what you know, but who you know" continues to hold significant weight in today's employment ecosystem.

Yet, the essence of networking extends beyond mere job hunting. It's about creating a fabric of **associations** that can support various facets of one's career and personal development. It involves **nurturing relationships** with care and genuine interest, which in turn creates a support system that can provide advice, feedback, and encouragement through the various phases of a career.

To excel in networking, one must approach it with strategy and sincerity. It requires a balance of giving and receiving, ensuring that the relationships built are not merely transactional but are grounded in **genuine engagement** and mutual respect. As we delve deeper into the subsequent chapters, we'll explore the specific strategies that can be employed to establish and sustain these valuable connections, enhancing not just professional trajectories but also enriching personal growth.

As we move forward, remember that the power of networking lies in its ability to open doors and create pathways that are not immediately visible. It is a skill that when mastered, can lead to a cascade of opportunities that enhance both professional and personal dimensions of life.

Overview of the Book

Embarking on this journey through **"Connective Career Crafting: Mastering the Art of Networking and Relationship Building for Professional Success,"** this book is meticulously designed to unfold layer by layer, the nuanced art of networking that transcends conventional methods and dives into the intricacies of establishing profound professional relationships. Aimed at empowering professionals across various stages of their careers, each chapter of this guide is structured to not only impart knowledge but also to inspire action and foster sustainable networking habits.

The book begins by laying the groundwork in **Chapter 1: The Foundations of Networking**, where I delve into what constitutes professional networking and its significant evolution over the decades. This chapter sets the stage by exploring historical contexts and defining the fundamental principles that form the bedrock of networking.

Moving forward, **Chapter 2: Mapping Your Existing Network** involves a hands-on approach where you'll learn to conduct a thorough inventory of your current connections and assess the strength of these ties. This chapter is crucial for understanding the existing resources within your reach and how to effectively leverage them.

In **Chapter 3: The Psychology Behind Effective Networking**, the focus shifts to the human element of networking. Here, the exploration into social dynamics within professional settings provides insights into building rapport and trust—essential components of lasting professional relationships.

Chapter 4: Networking Strategies for Career Growth introduces practical strategies for enhancing your networking efforts. From maximizing your presence at conferences and events to harnessing the power of social media and other online platforms, this chapter offers actionable steps for expanding your professional network.

Chapter 5: Mastering the Art of Communication highlights the critical role communication skills play in networking. It covers both verbal and non-verbal communication techniques, emphasizing the paramount importance of listening as a tool for building stronger connections.

The narrative progresses to **Chapter 6: Building and Maintaining Diverse Professional Relationships**, where the emphasis is on cultivating a diverse and robust network. This chapter discusses strategies for long-term relationship management, crucial for a thriving professional life.

Chapter 7: Networking Challenges and Solutions tackles the inevitable challenges that come with networking. From navigating common pitfalls to handling rejection and setbacks, this chapter prepares you to face and overcome these obstacles effectively.

Chapter 8: Advanced Networking Techniques explores the cutting-edge methods and technological tools available for networking in the digital age. Innovative approaches to connect with industry leaders are discussed, providing readers with the tools to stay ahead in a competitive landscape.

In **Chapter 9: Networking Success Stories**, real-world examples and case studies from various industries illustrate the transformative power of effective networking. This chapter analyzes successful networking strategies and the impact they can have on one's career.

Finally, **Chapter 10: Your Personal Networking Plan** helps you put all the knowledge into practice. It guides you in crafting a personalized networking strategy and provides tools and resources to kickstart your networking journey.

As this guide comes to a close, the **Conclusion** reflects on the key points discussed throughout the book and provides encouragement for ongoing networking efforts. The appendices include practical templates for networking outreach and a list of recommended reading and resources to further support your networking endeavors.

Through **"Connective Career Crafting,"** it is my goal to equip you with the knowledge and tools necessary to weave a network that not only advances your career but also enriches your professional and personal life. Each chapter is crafted with care, ensuring it serves as a stepping stone towards mastering the art of networking and relationship building. Embrace these principles and strategies, and you will find yourself well on your way to crafting a successful, interconnected career.

Chapter 1: The Foundations of Networking

Defining Professional Networking

In the fabric of career advancement, the concept of professional networking emerges as a cornerstone, pivotal for forging paths and unlocking doors to new opportunities. Before delving deeper into the strategies and nuances of networking, it's essential to establish a clear and comprehensive understanding of what professional networking truly entails.

Professional networking, at its core, is the deliberate activity of creating and maintaining relationships with people who can potentially help in your career development and professional growth. It is a strategic effort to connect with individuals and groups within and beyond your current industry or sector, who share similar professional interests or goals, or who possess the expertise and influence that can be mutually beneficial.

The essence of networking is not simply in accumulating contacts; rather, it is in fostering meaningful relationships that provide reciprocal benefits over time. This involves more than just exchanging business cards or connecting on professional social media platforms; it requires engaging in meaningful dialogues, sharing insights, and contributing to the development of each other's careers.

At its best, professional networking serves multiple purposes:

- **Information Exchange**: Networking provides a platform for the exchange of vital information about job opportunities, industry trends, and best practices. This exchange is invaluable as it offers insights that are not readily accessible through formal channels.

- **Opportunity Gateway**: Many career opportunities, especially those in the hidden job market, are often accessed through networking. Being well-connected opens doors to recommendations, referrals, and insider information about upcoming projects or vacancies.

- **Skill Enhancement**: Regular interaction with diverse professionals helps in honing communication and interpersonal skills. It also encourages continuous learning and adaptation to various professional environments.

- **Support System**: A robust network acts as a support system, offering advice, mentorship, and feedback. It can play a crucial role during career transitions, challenging projects, or when making strategic career decisions.

- **Reputation Building**: Effective networking helps in building and maintaining a professional reputation. Being known and visible in professional circles can lead to higher credibility and recognition in your field.

To engage in professional networking effectively, one must approach it with intentionality and authenticity. This involves being proactive in reaching out, showing genuine interest in the careers of your contacts, and looking for ways to be helpful without immediate expectations of returns. It's about building trust and rapport over time, which are the bedrocks of any strong professional relationship.

Moreover, networking is an evolving process. As industries change and professional journeys progress, the networks you build must also adapt and expand. It involves continuous effort to meet new people, reconnect with old acquaintances, and sometimes, step out of your comfort zone to attend gatherings and events that may not directly align with your current career path.

In embracing professional networking, remember that it is a two-way street. The value of your network is not just in the number of people you know, but in the quality of the relationships you maintain and the synergy you can create together. As this book unfolds, the subsequent chapters will guide you through various strategies to cultivate and nurture these relationships, ensuring your networking efforts are as effective and fulfilling as possible.

Navigating through the journey of professional networking requires more than just knowing the right people; it demands a commitment to growing and contributing to a community of professionals. Let's move forward, armed with a clear understanding of networking, to explore how to effectively apply these principles in real-world settings, transforming connections into valuable career assets.

Historical Perspective and Evolution

The art of networking, while a modern term, is grounded in practices as ancient as human society itself. Understanding the historical perspective and evolution of networking provides valuable insights into its enduring importance and the transformative ways it has shaped professional landscapes throughout the centuries.

The genesis of professional networking can be traced back to the guilds of the Middle Ages, which were associations of artisans or merchants who controlled the practice of their craft in a particular town. These early networks were not only crucial for business and trade but also served as vital support systems, providing members with socioeconomic safety nets.

As we moved into the Renaissance and Enlightenment periods, the focus of networking shifted towards the salons of Paris and the coffeehouses of London—places where intellectuals, artists, and scientists gathered. These settings were informal yet powerful networks, facilitating the exchange of ideas that spurred innovations and influenced political and cultural climates. Here, the foundation of networking as a catalyst for intellectual and cultural exchange was solidified.

The Industrial Revolution introduced another shift, emphasizing more structured professional networks that aligned with rapid industrial and economic growth. During this period, professional societies and chambers of commerce emerged, formalizing the process of networking and extending its reach beyond local communities to national and international spheres.

In the 20th century, the proliferation of corporations and the rise of the managerial class brought networking to the forefront of business strategy. The concept of "who you know" became as important as "what you know," with professional associations, alumni groups, and trade shows becoming key networking hubs. These platforms helped individuals gain a competitive edge in the increasingly complex and dynamic job market.

The late 20th and early 21st centuries have seen a significant transformation in networking, propelled by the digital revolution. The advent of the Internet and, subsequently, social media platforms like LinkedIn, Twitter, and Facebook, has radically expanded the scope and accessibility of professional networking. These digital tools have democratized networking, allowing individuals to connect across geographic and socio-economic boundaries with unprecedented ease.

Today, professional networking continues to evolve with emerging technologies such as artificial intelligence and blockchain reshaping how connections are formed and maintained. Virtual reality conferences and digital workspaces are becoming more commonplace, suggesting that the future of networking will increasingly rely on technology to simulate real-world interaction in an increasingly virtual professional environment.

Throughout its history, the essence of networking has remained consistent: it is about forging connections that foster mutual growth and advancement. The methods and scopes of networking may have evolved, but its core purpose—creating a community of shared interests and mutual benefits—remains unchanged. This historical perspective not only enriches our understanding of the concept but also underscores the adaptability and enduring relevance of networking in professional development.

As we continue to navigate through this book, let's keep in mind the lessons learned from the past and the possibilities that lie ahead. Networking, as demonstrated through history, is not just about building contacts but about building a community that transcends time and space, continually adapting to meet new challenges and seize new opportunities. Let this legacy inspire us to embrace modern networking strategies with an appreciation of their deep-rooted historical significance.

Chapter 2: Mapping Your Existing Network

Inventory of Current Connections

As we dive into the practical aspects of networking, one of the first and most critical steps is to take a comprehensive inventory of your current connections. This process is not merely about listing names and contact information; it involves a thorough analysis of who you know, how you know them, and the quality of those relationships. Understanding your existing network is foundational in recognizing its potential to aid in your professional growth and in identifying gaps that need bridging.

Conducting a thorough inventory begins with categorizing your connections into various groups based on the context in which you met them: professional settings, educational institutions, volunteer activities, social gatherings, online platforms, and more. Within these categories, further refinement is needed by classifying connections into subgroups such as industry, expertise, influence level, and the nature of your relationship (mentor, peer, acquaintance).

To systematically record and assess this information, leveraging a tool or a method is essential. Many professionals find it beneficial to use a digital spreadsheet or a specialized CRM (Customer Relationship Management) tool tailored for networking purposes. These tools allow you to not only list details but also to add notes on the frequency of your interactions, the mutual benefits of the relationship, and any specific anecdotes or interests that could serve as conversation starters in future interactions.

Evaluating the strength of each connection is crucial. This involves reflecting on the level of mutual trust, the history of past interactions, and the exchange of value between both parties. A strong connection is typically characterized by frequent interactions, mutual respect, and a history of collaborative or supportive exchanges. Conversely, weaker connections might need more nurturing to develop into valuable professional relationships.

Here's a more detailed look at how to evaluate and categorize your connections:

- **Core Connections**: These are individuals you trust implicitly, who likely know your professional capabilities deeply, and with whom you interact regularly. They are often your primary source of advice, mentorship, and support.

- **Strong Connections**: This group includes professionals with whom you do not interact as frequently but who you can rely on for significant support when needed. These connections are often cultivated through consistent, meaningful interactions over time.

- **Casual Connections**: These are individuals you know on a superficial level; perhaps you've met through conferences or have had brief interactions with them on social media. While the relationship might not be deep, it holds potential for development.

- **Dormant Connections**: These are past colleagues or contacts with whom you have lost touch. Reviving these connections can often lead to new opportunities, as both parties bring fresh experiences and insights into the rekindled relationship.

Taking inventory also means identifying **gaps in your network**. For instance, if you are looking to move into a new industry or gain expertise in a new area, you may discover that you lack connections in those sectors. Or perhaps you have many peers in your network but few mentors or influencers. Identifying these gaps allows you to strategically seek new connections that can offer the insights, mentorship, or opportunities you need.

Lastly, this inventory is not a one-time task; it's a dynamic component of your career strategy that should be revisited and updated regularly. As your career goals evolve, so too should your network. This ongoing process ensures that your networking efforts are aligned with your current and future professional aspirations.

By taking a detailed inventory of your current connections, you set the stage for deliberate networking efforts that are not only strategic but also tailored to your specific career goals. This foundational work is critical in transforming your network into a powerful asset for career development, opening doors to opportunities and facilitating growth in ways that would otherwise remain unexploited. Let's harness this knowledge to expand and enhance your professional landscape, making every connection count towards your ultimate career success.

Assessing the Strength of Your Ties

After meticulously cataloging your current connections, the next step is to assess the strength of those ties, which is crucial for effectively leveraging your network to support your professional aspirations. This assessment not only helps you understand who can offer the most relevant support and insight for your goals but also guides you in nurturing these relationships thoughtfully and strategically.

Understanding the strength of a connection involves evaluating several key aspects: the level of trust, the frequency and quality of interactions, the reciprocal nature of the relationship, and the relevance of the connection to your current and future professional needs.

1. **Level of Trust**: Trust is the cornerstone of any strong relationship. Assessing this involves reflecting on past interactions and whether those interactions have been consistent, reliable, and genuine. High trust is typically evident when there is a history of shared confidences, mutual respect, and direct honesty in your communications.

2. **Frequency and Quality of Interactions**: Regular contact helps strengthen relationships. Evaluate how often you engage with each connection, whether through face-to-face meetings, phone calls, emails, or social media interactions. Quality of interaction is equally important—consider whether these interactions are substantive and engaging or merely superficial.

3. **Reciprocity**: Effective networking is inherently reciprocal. Consider whether there is a balanced exchange of information, support, and resources. A strong tie will likely be characterized by a give-and-take dynamic where both parties benefit from the relationship.

4. **Relevance**: Assess how relevant each connection is to your professional field or your career goals. This involves considering whether a connection can provide industry insights, introduce you to key influencers, or support your professional development with advice and guidance.

Methods to Assess the Strength of Your Network

- **Relationship Mapping**: Visualizing your network can be incredibly useful. Create a visual map that categorizes your contacts based on the strength criteria mentioned above. Tools like network mapping software or even a simple spreadsheet can help organize this information effectively.

- **Interaction Tracking**: Keeping a record of interactions can help you gauge the frequency and quality of your engagements. Note the dates of interactions and brief points about what was discussed. Over time, patterns will emerge that highlight which connections are most engaged and supportive.

- **Feedback Solicitation**: Sometimes, direct feedback from your contacts can provide insights into the strength of your connections. This can be done through informal conversations where you discuss the relationship's mutual benefits, or more formally through feedback forms after collaborative projects or meetings.

- **Mutual Benefit Analysis**: Regularly review what you have offered to and received from each connection. This could include advice, introductions, business opportunities, and more. A healthy, strong relationship will often have a fairly equal balance, indicating a robust connection.

Strategic Application of This Assessment

Armed with a detailed understanding of the strengths and weaknesses of your network ties, you can strategically focus your efforts on nurturing the most beneficial relationships. Prioritize connections that offer the highest mutual value and align most closely with your career goals. For weaker ties, develop a strategy to strengthen these connections where it makes sense to do so, such as increasing your interaction frequency or finding new ways to provide value to those contacts.

Additionally, understanding the weaker parts of your network can highlight opportunities for growth—perhaps indicating areas where you might benefit from expanding your network to include more diverse perspectives or expertise.

This evaluation is not a one-time exercise but an ongoing part of professional development. As your career evolves, so too will the dynamics of your relationships. Continuously assessing and adjusting your network ensures that it remains a robust, responsive tool that can help navigate the complex terrain of professional growth and opportunity.

Through this iterative process of assessment and engagement, your network becomes not just a list of contacts, but a dynamic resource that evolves with your career, providing support, inspiration, and access to new opportunities. By leveraging the full potential of your connections, you pave the way for not just professional success but a rich, fulfilling professional journey.

Chapter 3: The Psychology Behind Effective Networking

Understanding Social Dynamics in Professional Settings

Navigating the landscape of professional settings requires a keen understanding of social dynamics—those unwritten rules and subtle cues that govern interactions in the workplace and beyond. This knowledge is not merely beneficial; it is essential for anyone looking to cultivate a successful career through networking. By grasping these dynamics, you can more effectively build rapport, foster trust, and create a network that supports and enhances your professional trajectory.

Social dynamics in professional settings involve a complex interplay of behavioral norms, cultural expectations, power structures, and interpersonal relationships. Understanding these elements can significantly influence your ability to communicate effectively and adapt your networking strategies to various environments.

1. **Behavioral Norms**: These are the accepted behaviors within a professional community. They can vary widely between industries,

companies, and even departments. Being attuned to these norms is crucial; it involves observing and mirroring the communication styles, dress codes, work ethics, and general professional conduct expected in different settings.

2. **Cultural Expectations**: Every organization and professional group has a culture that can deeply influence social interactions. This culture might prioritize collaboration over competition, value innovation, or uphold traditional business protocols. Understanding these cultural expectations is essential for anyone navigating these waters, as it allows for smoother interactions and enhances the chances of making meaningful connections.

3. **Power Structures**: Recognizing and understanding the hierarchy within professional settings can guide how you approach and interact with different individuals. Power structures often dictate who makes decisions, who influences those decisions, and how information flows within the network. Effective networkers know how to navigate these structures, identifying key influencers and decision-makers who can open doors and facilitate introductions.

4. **Interpersonal Relationships**: At the heart of networking lies the ability to form and maintain interpersonal relationships. This requires emotional intelligence, the capacity to empathize with others, and the skill to manage one's own emotions effectively. Successful networking is built on genuine connections that are nurtured over time, respecting each individual's boundaries and contributions.

Strategies to Master Social Dynamics in Professional Settings

- **Observation and Adaptation**: Spend time observing the interactions within a new group or setting before fully engaging. Note how leaders act, how colleagues interact, and how formal or informal the environment is. Adapt your behavior to fit seamlessly into the group while still maintaining your authentic self.

- **Cultural Competence**: Develop an awareness of the cultural backgrounds and preferences of your colleagues and business contacts. This sensitivity can greatly enhance interpersonal interactions and prevent misunderstandings. It shows respect and appreciation for diversity, which is highly valued in today's globalized business environment.

- **Strategic Engagement**: Identify the most influential people in your network and understand their roles within the power structure. Approach these individuals with respect and thoughtfulness, offering value and demonstrating genuine interest in their work.

- **Building Rapport**: Create connections by finding common ground and shared interests. This might involve discussing a mutual acquaintance, a shared hobby, or professional interests. Rapport building is an ongoing process and is crucial for turning superficial connections into deeper, more meaningful relationships.

- **Feedback and Reflection**: After networking events or interactions, reflect on what went well and what could be improved. Seek feedback from trusted colleagues or mentors who can provide insights into your interaction style and social effectiveness.

By mastering these social dynamics, you enhance your ability to navigate professional settings more confidently and effectively. These skills enable you to create and sustain relationships that are not only beneficial for your immediate career goals but also enrich your long-term professional journey. As you continue to engage with your network, keep these dynamics in mind, applying them thoughtfully to foster connections that are robust, supportive, and mutually beneficial. This understanding will serve as a foundation for all your networking endeavors, ensuring that each interaction contributes positively to your career path.

Building Rapport and Trust

In the realm of networking, building rapport and trust forms the bedrock upon which enduring and fruitful relationships are constructed. These elements are not just pivotal; they are essential to the formation of connections that transcend mere acquaintance, becoming instrumental in achieving profound professional success. The process of cultivating these vital components involves a strategic, empathetic, and consistent approach to every interaction within your network.

Rapport is the initial step to creating a comfortable and harmonious connection where both parties feel understood, respected, and valued. It is often cultivated through shared experiences, common interests, and a genuine sense of curiosity about the other person's background, challenges, and aspirations. Building rapport is an art that requires attentiveness, adaptability, and most importantly, authenticity.

Trust, on the other hand, evolves over time. It is the deeper fabric that binds relationships, ensuring that interactions are not only pleasant but also deeply reliable and imbued with integrity. Trust is built through consistent actions, ethical behavior, and a proven track record of respecting confidences and following through on commitments.

Strategies for Building Rapport

- **Active Listening**: Truly listening to others is perhaps the most critical skill in building rapport. It involves not just hearing words but also understanding the emotions and intentions behind them. This means engaging fully, asking insightful questions, and reflecting back what you have heard to show understanding and interest.

- **Mirroring Language and Behavior**: Subtly mirroring the language, tone, and body language of the person you are speaking with can create a subliminal sense of alignment and agreement. This should be done carefully and naturally to ensure it reinforces a genuine connection rather than coming across as mimicry.

- **Finding Common Ground**: Discover shared interests or common professional challenges. This could be as simple as discussing a mutual hobby, a shared professional acquaintance, or common industry trends. Shared experiences are the pillars upon which rapport is built.

- **Showing Genuine Interest**: Show that you are interested in more than just a professional advantage. Express curiosity about their projects, achievements, and professional journeys. This personal attention can set the foundation for a relationship that feels both supportive and collaborative.

Strategies for Building Trust

- **Consistency in Actions**: Be reliable in your interactions and follow through on what you say you will do. Whether it is returning a call, delivering a document, or providing an introduction, consistency establishes your reputation as trustworthy.

- **Transparency and Honesty**: Be open about your intentions and be honest in your communications. If you seek advice, be clear about it. If you are offering help, let it be known why you are doing so. Transparency fosters trust and can clear any potential misunderstandings.

- **Respecting Confidentiality**: When confidences are shared, respecting them is crucial. Trust can be rapidly destroyed by sharing or misusing confidential information. Demonstrating that you can be trusted with sensitive information reinforces your integrity.

- **Providing Value Selflessly**: Whenever possible, contribute first without an immediate expectation of return. Offering your expertise, making an introduction, or sharing a resource without immediately seeking something in return can significantly enhance trust.

- **Recovery from Missteps**: Inevitably, misunderstandings or errors may occur. Addressing these openly and seeking resolution promptly can actually strengthen trust, demonstrating your commitment to the relationship.

As you implement these strategies, it is crucial to maintain a balance between professional and personal interaction, ensuring that while the relationship may be professionally based, it is personally respectful and caring. This careful nurturing of both rapport and trust not only enriches your professional network but also enhances your overall career satisfaction and success.

By understanding and applying these principles, each connection you cultivate can become a pillar of your ongoing professional journey, supporting not just your career growth but also contributing to a robust and dynamic industry community. As we move forward, let these strategies guide your interactions, turning every handshake into a meaningful exchange and every conversation into a step toward mutual success.

Chapter 4: Networking Strategies for Career Growth

Strategic Networking at Conferences and Events

Conferences and professional events serve as dynamic platforms for strategic networking, offering unique opportunities to connect with a diverse array of industry leaders, potential mentors, and peers who can profoundly impact your career trajectory. These gatherings are not merely about attending; they are about engaging strategically, with clear goals and a plan of action that maximizes every interaction.

Preparation is key when approaching networking opportunities at conferences and events. Prior to attending, it's essential to research the event thoroughly: understand its theme, know the key speakers, and identify the attendees who align with your professional interests and goals. Setting specific objectives for whom you want to meet and what you hope to achieve lays a solid foundation for effective networking.

Effective Tactics for Conference Networking

- **Plan Your Approach**: Before the event, reach out to key individuals you aim to connect with. A brief, polite email introducing yourself and expressing interest in discussing common professional interests can pave the way for a face-to-face conversation during the event.

- **Utilize the Agenda**: Familiarize yourself with the schedule to strategically attend sessions that are most relevant to your goals. This targeted approach not only enhances your learning but also places you in the same room with professionals who share your interests, making conversations more relevant and engaging.

- **Elevator Pitch**: Have a concise, compelling self-introduction ready. Your elevator pitch should communicate who you are, what you do, and what value you bring to your professional circle. It should be adaptable, allowing you to highlight aspects of your background that are most relevant to each new connection.

- **Active Participation**: Engage actively by asking questions during sessions, participating in discussions, and contributing your insights. Visibility is a key component of networking; when you contribute thoughtfully, you position yourself as a knowledgeable and engaged professional.

- **Social Gatherings**: Don't underestimate the power of social events associated with conferences. These less formal environments can be perfect for initiating conversations in a more relaxed setting, making it easier to form genuine connections.

- **Follow-Up**: After the event, prompt follow-up is crucial. Send personalized emails or LinkedIn messages referencing specific details from your conversations. This not only reinforces your interest but also keeps the lines of communication open for future interactions.

Leveraging Technology and Social Media

In today's digital age, the integration of technology and social media into conference networking can significantly enhance your ability to connect with others. Prior to attending, engaging with the event's social media pages, using the official hashtags, or participating in pre-event webinars can increase your visibility and establish initial contact points.

During the event, many conferences offer dedicated apps that facilitate networking by allowing attendees to schedule meetings, join interest-based groups, and participate in discussions. Utilizing these tools can help you manage your time effectively and enhance your networking experience.

Networking with a Purpose

Remember, the goal of networking at conferences and events is not merely to collect business cards or add connections on LinkedIn. It is about building meaningful relationships that provide mutual value over time. Each interaction should be approached with the intent to listen, learn, and contribute, ensuring that the connections you make are both authentic and beneficial.

As you navigate these professional gatherings, keep in mind that every handshake, every exchange, and every follow-up is a step towards building a robust professional network that supports your career aspirations. Conferences and events offer a unique convergence of minds and talents—make sure you are prepared to dive into this pool of opportunities, armed with a strategy, a smile, and a sincere interest in the people you meet.

By adopting these strategies, you transform each event attendance into a significant opportunity for career development, leveraging the collective expertise and potential of your professional community to propel your career forward. Let these experiences be more than just meetings; let them be the catalysts for long-lasting professional relationships and career milestones.

Leveraging Social Media and Online Platforms

In today's interconnected world, mastering the art of networking extends well beyond in-person interactions. Social media and online platforms have become pivotal tools in building and sustaining professional relationships. These digital environments offer unprecedented opportunities to reach out to industry leaders, share expertise, and stay updated on market trends and opportunities. Understanding how to effectively leverage these platforms is essential for anyone looking to enhance their professional visibility and connectivity.

Crafting a Professional Online Presence: The first step in leveraging social media for networking is to create a polished, professional online presence. Platforms like LinkedIn, Twitter, and even industry-specific forums allow you to showcase your professional background, achievements, and areas of expertise. Your profiles on these platforms should be carefully curated to reflect your professional identity and goals. This includes a professional photo, a compelling bio, and a clear articulation of your career interests and skills.

Engaging with Content and Communities: Once your profiles are set up, actively engage with content relevant to your field. This can be achieved by following industry leaders, joining professional groups, and participating in discussions. Posting regularly and sharing insightful articles, thought leadership pieces, and updates about your professional journey helps establish your voice in the community. Commenting on posts and contributing to conversations not only increases your visibility but also demonstrates your knowledge and eagerness to engage with peers.

Networking Through LinkedIn: LinkedIn is particularly powerful for building professional connections. Regularly update your profile with new skills, endorsements, and professional experiences. Utilize LinkedIn's features like recommendations to gain credibility, and endorsements to validate your skills. Engage with your connections by congratulating them on new jobs, commenting on their posts, or sharing relevant information. LinkedIn also allows for more targeted networking efforts through the use of InMail, enabling you to reach out directly to people you do not yet know personally but wish to connect with professionally.

Twitter for Real-time Engagement: Twitter offers a more dynamic platform for networking, allowing you to engage in real-time conversations about current events in your industry. Use hashtags relevant to your field to join broader conversations, follow conferences or live events, and connect with thought leaders. Retweeting, quoting, and replying to tweets are effective ways to engage with content and contributors, thereby increasing your own profile's engagement and visibility.

Utilizing Online Forums and Industry Groups: Beyond LinkedIn and Twitter, many professions have specific online communities where members share advice, job postings, and industry news. Participating in these forums not only helps you gain valuable insights but also establishes you as an active member of your professional community. Engage genuinely, offer advice when you can, and ask thoughtful questions.

Blogs and Personal Websites: Maintaining a professional blog or a personal website can further enhance your online presence. Regularly publishing high-quality content that addresses current trends, challenges, or innovations in your field can position you as a thought leader. Sharing these posts across your social media platforms drives traffic to your site and sparks conversations that can lead to new connections.

Privacy and Professionalism: While engaging on these platforms, always maintain a high level of professionalism. Be mindful of the information you share and keep your interactions positive and respectful. Privacy settings should be managed to ensure that what you are comfortable sharing is visible to the right audiences, protecting your personal information while still being open enough to foster connections.

In conclusion, social media and online platforms are not just tools for communication—they are essential channels for building and nurturing professional relationships in today's digital age. By strategically leveraging these platforms, you can expand your network far beyond what traditional networking would allow, accessing global opportunities and connections that are transformative not only for your career but also for your professional development. This digital approach to networking, when done thoughtfully and consistently, can significantly amplify your professional reach and impact. As we move forward, embrace these digital tools to craft a network that supports your career goals, ensuring that each online interaction brings you one step closer to professional success.

Chapter 5: Mastering the Art of Communication

Verbal and Non-verbal Communication Skills

Effective communication is the cornerstone of successful networking. It's not merely about what is said but how it is said and what is communicated non-verbally. Mastering both verbal and non-verbal communication skills can dramatically enhance your ability to build meaningful and productive professional relationships.

Verbal Communication: This involves the words you choose, the tone of your voice, and the clarity of your message. Every interaction provides an opportunity to make a positive impression through articulate, thoughtful communication.

- **Clarity and Brevity**: Be clear and concise in your communication. Avoid jargon unless it is common in the listener's field, and always aim to convey your thoughts in a straightforward manner. This ensures that your ideas are understood and remembered.

- **Tone of Voice**: The tone conveys your attitude and can significantly affect how your message is received. A friendly, confident tone can make you more approachable and encourage open communication.

- **Active Language**: Use active verbs and a positive tone to convey energy and engagement. This makes your conversation more compelling and can help maintain the listener's interest.

Non-verbal Communication: Often, how you say something is more impactful than what you say. Non-verbal cues like body language, facial expressions, and eye contact play a crucial role in communicating your message and emotional intent.

- **Body Language**: Open body language (uncrossed arms, relaxed posture, leaning slightly forward) can make you appear more approachable and engaged. In contrast, closed body language (crossed arms, avoiding eye contact) might suggest disinterest or discomfort.

- **Facial Expressions**: Your expressions can convey a wealth of emotions and should be congruent with your words. Smiling, for instance, typically shows warmth and openness, making others more comfortable in your presence.

- **Eye Contact**: Maintaining appropriate eye contact shows confidence and sincerity. It encourages trust and shows that you are fully engaged in the interaction.

Integrating Verbal and Non-verbal Skills: The most effective communicators skillfully integrate verbal and non-verbal communication. This synchronization makes interactions more genuine and impactful. For instance, if you are discussing a serious topic, your tone should be sober and your body language should reflect the seriousness of the subject.

Practicing Communication Skills

- **Role-playing**: Practice your communication skills with a friend or mentor, and ask for feedback. Role-playing different networking scenarios can help you refine your approach before you engage in actual professional settings.

- **Recording and Reviewing**: Consider recording your practice sessions to identify areas of strength and those needing improvement. Pay attention to your verbal ticks and non-verbal habits.

- **Continual Learning**: Enroll in workshops or seminars that focus on communication skills.

These can provide valuable insights and strategies for effective speaking and presentation, which are beneficial in networking contexts.

- **Mindfulness and Adaptation**: Be mindful of the cultural context of your communications. Different cultures have varying norms regarding verbal and non-verbal communications. Adapt your style to suit the cultural expectations and comfort levels of your audience to enhance understanding and rapport.

In conclusion, mastering both verbal and non-verbal communication is essential for successful networking. These skills enable you to express yourself more effectively, build rapport more quickly, and create a lasting impression on those you meet. As you progress in your career, continually refining these skills will open doors to new opportunities and deeper professional relationships, laying a solid foundation for ongoing success. Let each conversation you engage in be a step toward building stronger, more effective connections within your professional network.

Listening: The Key to Successful Networking

In the intricate dance of networking, listening is perhaps the most crucial step, yet it is often the most overlooked. Effective listening goes beyond simply hearing words; it involves understanding, interpreting, and responding thoughtfully to both the verbal and non-verbal messages people convey. This chapter delves deep into the art of listening, a skill that not only enhances your ability to connect with others but also fundamentally strengthens your professional relationships.

The Importance of Active Listening in Networking

Active listening is engaging with the speaker to understand their message thoroughly. It is about focusing completely on the speaker, understanding their message, responding appropriately, and then remembering what was said. In networking contexts, active listening can transform casual conversations into lasting connections because it shows that you value not just the relationship but also the person behind it.

- **Engagement and Empathy**: Active listening is characterized by a genuine interest in the other person's words. It involves empathy, where you try to see the world from the speaker's perspective. This can be particularly impactful in networking, as it helps build a rapport based on genuine understanding and concern.

- **Building Trust**: When people feel heard, they are more likely to trust you. Trust is the cornerstone of any meaningful professional relationship. By listening attentively, you signal that you are trustworthy and respectful of others' ideas and opinions.

- **Facilitating Mutual Exchange**: Good listening ensures that the conversation is a two-way street. It invites open communication and makes the other person feel comfortable sharing ideas, advice, and opportunities.

Techniques for Enhancing Listening Skills

- **Maintain Eye Contact**: Eye contact is a powerful way of showing attentiveness. It tells the speaker that you are fully concentrated on the conversation. However, be mindful of cultural differences in eye contact norms, as direct eye contact is not considered appropriate in some cultures.

- **Use Non-verbal Cues**: Nodding your head, leaning slightly forward, or showing expressions that match the conversation's emotional tone can all signal that you are engaged in the conversation.

- **Avoid Interrupting**: Allow the speaker to finish their thoughts before responding. Interrupting can signal impatience and a lack of respect for the speaker's opinions.

- **Clarify and Confirm**: Paraphrase what has been said to confirm understanding. Ask clarifying questions to delve deeper into the subject or to clear up any ambiguities.

- **Remember Key Details**: Make a mental note of important details mentioned during the conversation. Referencing these details in future interactions can greatly enhance the personal connection, showing that you were truly listening and that you value the relationship.

Listening in Different Contexts

The ability to adjust your listening style according to the context is an invaluable skill. For instance, in a casual networking event, your listening style can be more relaxed and open-ended, encouraging a free flow of ideas. In a more formal setting, such as a professional meeting, your listening should be more focused and driven, with an emphasis on extracting key information.

- **Digital Communication**: In online interactions, listening can take the form of carefully reading messages and responding thoughtfully. Pay attention to the tone and content of emails or messages, which can often convey more than the words might suggest.

- **Feedback and Continuous Improvement**: Seek feedback on your listening skills from trusted peers or mentors. Use this feedback to continuously improve how you engage in conversations.

Effective listening is much more than a passive activity; it is an active, dynamic process that enriches your understanding and enhances your professional relationships. By mastering the art of listening, you equip yourself with a tool that is both subtle and powerful, helping you to navigate the complex world of professional networking with grace and efficiency. Let your listening skills open doors to deeper insights, stronger relationships, and more meaningful opportunities in your career journey.

Chapter 6: Building and Maintaining Diverse Professional Relationships

Cultivating a Diverse Network

In today's globalized economy, the ability to cultivate a diverse network is more than a strategic advantage—it is a necessity. Diversity in networking not only broadens your perspective and access to a variety of resources but also enhances creativity and innovation in your professional dealings. A diverse network, encompassing a wide range of skills, experiences, and backgrounds, can act as a powerful catalyst for growth and opportunity in ways that a homogeneous network cannot.

Why Diversity Matters in Professional Networking

Diversity in a professional network means more than just connecting with people from different industries or professions. It encompasses age, ethnicity, gender, cultural backgrounds, and even differing schools of thought. Each individual brings a unique set of experiences and knowledge that can provide new insights, challenge your thinking, and introduce you to new concepts, tools, and strategies.

- **Enhanced Problem Solving**: Studies have shown that diverse groups are better at problem solving. Different perspectives lead to a more thorough exploration of potential solutions, resulting in more effective outcomes.

- **Innovation and Creativity**: Exposure to a variety of perspectives encourages innovative thinking. People from different backgrounds can inspire new ideas and creative solutions to common problems.

- **Expanded Opportunities**: A diverse network can open doors to new markets, industries, and cultural insights that can be crucial for business expansion or career transitions.

Strategies for Building a Diverse Network

- **Attend Varied Networking Events**: Actively seek out and participate in networking events that attract a diverse audience. Industry conferences, webinars, workshops, and community social events are potential venues where you can meet people from different backgrounds.

- **Leverage Social Media Platforms**: Use platforms like LinkedIn to connect with professionals from a range of industries and cultural backgrounds. Join groups that are outside of your immediate professional circle to gain insights into other fields and practices.

- **Engage in Cross-Disciplinary Projects**: Participate in projects that require a multidisciplinary approach. These projects can provide access to professionals with different skill sets and perspectives, enriching your professional experience and expanding your network.

- **Promote Inclusivity in Your Existing Network**: Encourage and facilitate connections among your current contacts. Creating a more interconnected network can foster opportunities for collaboration and innovation among your peers.

- **Mentorship and Reverse Mentorship**: Engage in mentorship opportunities where you can learn from someone younger or from a different background (reverse mentorship). This can be particularly enlightening, as it opens you up to current trends and new technologies that you might not be familiar with.

- **Continued Education and Self-Improvement**: Enroll in courses or workshops that are outside your comfort zone. Education is a powerful tool for broadening your horizons and meeting people who think differently.

The Impact of a Diverse Network

A well-cultivated, diverse network allows for a more robust exchange of ideas, access to a broader range of job opportunities, and stronger, more innovative professional relationships. It challenges you to think critically and creatively, pushing beyond the boundaries of traditional solutions.

Moreover, a diverse network reflects the complex, interconnected world in which we live and work today. It prepares you to operate more effectively within this world, equipping you with the understanding and skills necessary to navigate various cultural and professional landscapes.

In essence, the effort to expand and diversify your network is an investment in your career's resilience and adaptability. It ensures that you remain relevant and effective in a rapidly changing global market. As we move forward, let this focus on diversity guide your networking strategy, enriching not only your professional life but also contributing to a more inclusive and dynamic professional environment. Through these efforts, your network will become a true reflection of the world's diversity, brimming with opportunities for growth, learning, and collaboration.

Long-Term Relationship Management

In the journey of professional networking, the initial connection is merely the beginning. The true art lies in nurturing these relationships over time, transforming fleeting interactions into enduring alliances that support and enrich both parties. Effective long-term relationship management is not about merely keeping in touch; it involves continuous engagement, mutual benefit, and genuine interest in the growth and success of those within your network.

The Foundations of Sustaining Professional Relationships

Long-term relationship management starts with the understanding that every professional relationship can be a bridge to new opportunities—not just for you but for your connections as well. This reciprocal nature of networking is crucial; it involves giving as much as you take, often more. Here are foundational strategies for ensuring that your professional relationships are enduring and mutually beneficial:

- **Regular Communication**: Consistency is key. Regular updates, whether through emails, social media messages, or phone calls, help keep the relationship alive. These communications don't always have to be about seeking favors; sharing interesting articles, congratulating them on personal achievements, or simply checking in can keep the bond strong.

- **Add Value**: Always look for ways to add value to your connections. This could be in the form of providing a resource, offering your expertise, or introducing them to another contact who could help with their goals. By being a valuable resource, you cement your position as a key figure in their professional life.

- **Celebrate Milestones**: Acknowledge and celebrate the successes of your connections. Whether it's a new job, a business launch, or a personal milestone, showing that you care about their achievements fosters a deeper connection and mutual respect.

- **Seek Feedback and Provide Support**: Be open to receiving and giving feedback. Supporting your connections in times of need—such as offering advice during career transitions or providing recommendations—strengthens the relationship.

- **Relevance and Respect**: As careers evolve, so do professional needs and interests. Stay relevant by updating your knowledge about your connections' shifting professional landscapes and by respecting their time and contributions.

Advanced Strategies for Long-Term Relationship Management

To take your relationship management to the next level, consider the following advanced strategies:

- **Personalized Interactions**: Customize your interactions based on the specific history and preferences of each connection. Remember details from previous conversations and follow up on specific points discussed. This personalized approach shows attentiveness and respect for the individual relationship.

- **Scheduled Check-ins**: Use digital tools to remind you of important dates in your connections' professional lives, such as work anniversaries or the launch of a new project. Scheduling regular check-ins can help you maintain contact without overwhelming your connections or yourself.

- **Networking Events Revisited**: Whenever possible, reconnect in person. Invite connections to relevant events or arrange meet-ups at industry conferences. Face-to-face interactions can rejuvenate relationships and provide a more personal touch.

- **Leveraging Technology**: Utilize CRM (Customer Relationship Management) tools or networking apps designed to manage professional relationships. These tools can help track interactions, notes, and important personal data to keep your outreach efforts organized and timely.

- **Continuous Learning and Adaptation**: Stay informed about best practices in networking and relationship management. The landscape of professional interaction is constantly evolving with technology and cultural shifts; staying adaptable is essential.

Conclusion

Long-term relationship management is an art that requires patience, consistency, and genuine interest in the welfare of others. It's about building a network that not only serves professional purposes but also contributes to a rich, supportive, and vibrant professional ecosystem. As you foster these relationships, remember that each connection has the potential to change not just your career trajectory but also the paths of those within your network. Let this understanding guide your interactions, turning every connection into a lasting partnership and every professional endeavor into a shared success.

Chapter 7: Networking Challenges and Solutions

Common Pitfalls and How to Avoid Them

Navigating the complex world of professional networking involves more than just building connections; it also requires avoiding common pitfalls that can undermine your efforts to forge meaningful relationships. Awareness of these potential missteps, coupled with strategic planning, can significantly enhance the efficacy of your networking activities and safeguard your professional reputation.

Overlooking Follow-Up

One of the most common mistakes in networking is failing to follow up after initial contacts. Whether it's a brief meeting at a conference or a formal business encounter, the lack of follow-up can lead to missed opportunities and give the impression of disinterest.

- **Strategy for Avoidance**: Always send a personalized follow-up message or email within 24 to 48 hours of a meeting. Express gratitude for the time spent, reference specific points from the conversation, and propose a next step or future meeting if relevant.

Focusing Too Much on Quantity Over Quality

While expanding your network is important, an excessive focus on quantity over quality can dilute the strength of your connections. This approach often leads to superficial relationships that lack depth and genuine mutual benefit.

- **Strategy for Avoidance**: Prioritize the depth and relevance of connections over sheer numbers. Invest time in getting to know people and nurturing those relationships. Quality connections are more likely to provide value and support over the long term.

Neglecting Diverse Connections

Ignoring the power of a diverse network is a significant oversight. Diversity in networking means including people from different industries, backgrounds, and experience levels, which can enrich your understanding and expose you to new perspectives and opportunities.

- **Strategy for Avoidance**: Actively seek out individuals whose backgrounds or careers differ from your own. Attend varied networking events, join different professional groups, and engage in communities outside your immediate area of expertise.

Undervaluing Soft Skills

Networking isn't just about exchanging business cards or LinkedIn profiles; it's also about how you interact. Neglecting soft skills like active listening, empathy, and the ability to engage in meaningful conversations can hinder the development of strong relationships.

- **Strategy for Avoidance**: Continuously work on your communication skills, particularly listening and empathizing. Practice these skills in every interaction, and seek feedback to improve.

Being Overly Aggressive or Salesy

Approaching networking with an overly aggressive or sales-oriented demeanor can be off-putting. People prefer to connect with those who show genuine interest in them, not just those out to gain a quick advantage.

- **Strategy for Avoidance**: Approach networking with a mindset of building relationships, not just closing a deal. Focus on how you can help others before considering what they can do for you. This approach not only makes interactions more pleasant but also more likely to result in mutual benefits.

Lack of Preparation

Entering a networking situation without proper preparation can leave you floundering, unable to effectively communicate your goals or understand how best to interact with others.

- **Strategy for Avoidance**: Before attending any networking event or meeting, research the attendees, prepare talking points, and set clear objectives for what you want to achieve. Knowing who you're meeting and why will help you make the most of every interaction.

Failure to Adapt to Different Cultural Norms

In today's globalized professional environment, understanding and adapting to different cultural norms is crucial. Misunderstandings can occur if cultural differences are not respected.

- **Strategy for Avoidance**: Educate yourself about the cultural backgrounds of your contacts. Be mindful of cultural differences in communication styles, meeting etiquette, and business practices.

In conclusion, effective networking requires more than just connecting with others; it demands a thoughtful approach that considers the long-term development and maintenance of relationships. By being aware of these common pitfalls and actively working to avoid them, you can build a robust network that supports both your personal and professional growth. Let these strategies guide you in crafting meaningful connections that last, ensuring that each interaction contributes positively to your network's richness and diversity.

Dealing with Rejection and Setbacks

In the landscape of professional networking, not every effort yields immediate success. Rejection and setbacks are an inherent part of the networking process, often serving as critical learning points that pave the way for future growth. Understanding how to handle these moments with grace and resilience can transform potential negatives into powerful catalysts for development and refinement of your networking strategies.

Understanding the Nature of Rejection in Networking

Rejection, whether it's a declined connection request, an unanswered email, or an unproductive meeting, often feels personal. However, it's crucial to recognize that rejection in professional settings is rarely a reflection of personal worth or capability. More often, it relates to the current priorities, needs, or circumstances of the other party.

- **Temporal Misalignment**: Sometimes, the timing isn't right. The individual you're reaching out to may be focusing on other projects or facing personal challenges that limit their capacity to engage.

- **Misalignment of Interests**: At other times, there may be a lack of alignment in professional interests or goals. What you offer might not match what the other person needs at that moment.

Strategies for Overcoming and Learning from Rejection

- **Reflect and Learn**: Use rejection as a moment for reflection. Review your approach, consider the context of the interaction, and assess if there's anything you could improve, such as your communication tactics or the timing of your outreach.

- **Maintain Professionalism**: Always respond to rejection professionally. A courteous acknowledgment of a rejection can leave the door open for future opportunities. Express gratitude for their time and consideration, and express a wish to keep in touch.

- **Resilience and Persistence**: Resilience in the face of rejection involves not taking 'no' as a final answer but as a 'not now.' Maintain a positive outlook and persist with your networking efforts, adjusting your strategies as necessary.

- **Expand Your Network**: Broaden your networking efforts to include a wider array of prospects. This diversification can increase your chances of creating meaningful connections and reduce the impact of individual rejections.

- **Seek Feedback**: If possible, seek feedback from those who have declined your requests or offers. Understanding their reasons can provide valuable insights into your approach and help tailor your strategies to better align with your networking goals.

Long-Term Management of Setbacks

Handling setbacks in networking requires a strategic approach that focuses on long-term goals rather than immediate gains.

- **Cultivate Emotional Intelligence**: Developing emotional intelligence can greatly enhance your ability to deal with rejection and setbacks. Being aware of, controlling, and expressing one's emotions healthily helps maintain self-confidence and persistence in the face of challenges.

- **Adopt a Growth Mindset**: View each setback as an opportunity to learn and grow. A growth mindset encourages resilience, motivating you to keep pushing forward and refining your networking strategies.

- **Networking Support Groups**: Consider joining or forming support groups with fellow professionals who can provide advice, share experiences, and offer emotional support. These groups can be invaluable in helping navigate the highs and lows of networking.

In wrapping up, remember that dealing with rejection and setbacks is a normal part of any professional journey, especially within the realm of networking. The key to turning these experiences into positives lies in your response and ability to adapt and persevere. Let each challenge refine your approach, making you not only a more skilled networker but also a more resilient professional. Embrace these moments as essential steps on your path to success, knowing that each interaction, successful or not, is a building block in the architecture of your career.

Chapter 8: Advanced Networking Techniques

Utilizing Technology for Networking

In an age where digital connectivity has become the cornerstone of professional interactions, effectively leveraging technology for networking is no longer optional—it is essential. The digital landscape offers a plethora of tools and platforms that can amplify your networking efforts, enabling you to build, manage, and nurture relationships with unprecedented efficiency and reach. Understanding and mastering these technological tools can dramatically enhance your networking capabilities, opening doors to opportunities that might otherwise remain inaccessible.

The Role of Social Media in Professional Networking

Social media platforms such as LinkedIn, Twitter, and Facebook have revolutionized the way professionals connect. LinkedIn, in particular, stands out as a premier platform designed specifically for professional networking. Here's how to utilize these platforms to their fullest potential:

- **LinkedIn**: Build a comprehensive and compelling profile that highlights your skills, experiences, and career achievements. Engage with your network by sharing relevant content, commenting on posts, and joining industry-specific groups. Utilize LinkedIn's advanced search functions to identify and connect with key industry figures. Regularly endorse skills and seek recommendations to build credibility.

- **Twitter**: Use Twitter to follow industry leaders, join professional conversations, and stay updated on industry trends. Engage with content by retweeting, liking, and replying to posts. Use hashtags strategically to join broader discussions and increase the visibility of your tweets.

- **Facebook**: While often seen as a more personal platform, Facebook can also be a valuable tool for professional networking through its groups and pages. Join professional groups related to your industry, participate in discussions, and use Facebook's event features to discover and attend networking events.

Professional Networking Apps

Several apps are designed to facilitate professional networking, making it easier to manage connections, schedule meetings, and discover new opportunities. Some of the most effective networking apps include:

- **Shapr**: This app operates like a professional version of Tinder, allowing you to swipe through profiles and connect with individuals who share your professional interests and goals.

- **Bumble Bizz**: Part of the Bumble app suite, Bumble Bizz focuses on networking for career opportunities. It allows you to create a profile showcasing your skills and experiences and match with potential connections in your area.

- **Meetup**: Use Meetup to find and join groups and events in your local area that align with your professional interests. It's a great way to meet people face-to-face and build lasting relationships.

Virtual Events and Webinars

The rise of virtual events and webinars has expanded the possibilities for networking beyond geographical limitations. Participating in these events can provide access to a global network of professionals.

- **Webinar Platforms**: Platforms like Zoom, GoToWebinar, and Microsoft Teams host a variety of webinars on diverse topics. Engaging in these sessions by asking questions, participating in discussions, and following up with speakers and attendees can lead to valuable connections.

- **Virtual Conferences**: Many industry conferences have moved online, offering virtual networking lounges, breakout sessions, and interactive Q&A panels. Take advantage of these features to interact with speakers and other attendees.

Email and CRM Tools

Managing a growing network can be challenging without the right tools. Customer Relationship Management (CRM) tools designed for networking can help keep track of your interactions and maintain relationships over time.

- **CRM Software**: Tools like HubSpot, Salesforce, and Zoho CRM allow you to manage contacts, schedule follow-ups, and track communications. These platforms can automate reminders and provide analytics to help you understand your networking patterns and opportunities.

- **Email Marketing**: Use email marketing tools like Mailchimp or Constant Contact to send regular updates, newsletters, or personalized messages to your network. Segment your contacts based on interests and engagement to tailor your communication effectively.

Innovative Networking Technologies

Emerging technologies continue to reshape the landscape of professional networking. Staying ahead of these trends can give you a significant advantage.

- **Artificial Intelligence (AI)**: AI-powered tools can help identify potential connections, suggest relevant content, and even automate initial outreach. Platforms like Crystal use AI to analyze personality traits and suggest communication strategies tailored to individual contacts.

- **Virtual Reality (VR)**: VR is starting to make its mark in networking, with platforms like AltspaceVR and VRChat hosting virtual networking events where participants can interact in a simulated environment. This can provide a more immersive and engaging networking experience.

Best Practices for Utilizing Technology in Networking

- **Consistency and Authenticity**: Regularly update your online profiles and engage consistently with your network. Authentic interactions build trust and establish stronger connections.

- **Personalization**: Tailor your messages and outreach efforts to the individual. Personalized communication demonstrates care and consideration, setting you apart in a sea of generic messages.

- **Follow Up and Follow Through**: Use technology to set reminders for follow-ups and track your commitments. Ensuring you follow through on promises builds credibility and strengthens relationships.

By harnessing the power of technology, you can expand your networking efforts far beyond traditional boundaries, creating a rich tapestry of connections that support your professional growth. As you integrate these digital tools into your networking strategy, remember that the core principles of genuine engagement and mutual benefit remain unchanged. Let technology enhance these principles, making your networking endeavors more efficient, expansive, and impactful.

Innovative Approaches to Connect with Industry Leaders

Connecting with industry leaders can significantly elevate your professional network, providing access to invaluable insights, mentorship, and opportunities that can propel your career forward. However, reaching out to these influential figures requires a strategic, thoughtful approach that sets you apart from the crowd. Traditional methods might get you a foot in the door, but innovative approaches can foster deeper connections and meaningful engagements.

Leveraging Content Creation

One of the most effective ways to capture the attention of industry leaders is through content creation. By establishing yourself as a thought leader in your own right, you can naturally attract the attention of those who are influential in your field.

- **Writing Articles and Blogs**: Publish articles or blogs on platforms like LinkedIn, Medium, or industry-specific websites. Focus on topics that are relevant to your industry and showcase your expertise. Share your content widely and tag industry leaders or reference their work within your articles to get on their radar.

- **Creating Videos and Podcasts**: Launch a YouTube channel or a podcast where you discuss industry trends, interview experts, and share your professional journey. Video and audio content can be more engaging than written content and can help you build a loyal audience, including industry leaders.

- **Social Media Engagement**: Actively engage with the content that industry leaders share on social media. Comment thoughtfully on their posts, share their articles, and contribute to discussions. This consistent engagement can help you build a relationship over time.

Hosting and Attending Webinars

Webinars offer a dual opportunity: they allow you to share your knowledge while also providing a platform to engage with industry leaders.

- **Hosting Webinars**: Organize webinars on topics within your expertise and invite industry leaders as guest speakers. This not only provides value to your audience but also gives you a direct line to influential figures. The collaborative nature of webinars can help build a strong professional relationship.

- **Attending Webinars**: Participate in webinars hosted by industry leaders. Engage actively by asking insightful questions and participating in discussions. Follow up with the hosts and speakers afterwards with personalized messages that reference the content of the webinar.

Utilizing Technology and Tools

Modern technology offers a variety of tools to facilitate networking with industry leaders. These tools can help you identify, reach out to, and maintain connections with influential figures in your field.

- **Professional Networking Apps**: Use apps like LinkedIn, Shapr, and Clubhouse to connect with industry leaders. LinkedIn's premium features, such as InMail, allow you to send direct messages to individuals outside your immediate network. Clubhouse, an audio-based social networking app, offers rooms where you can listen to and engage with industry leaders in real-time.

- **CRM Software**: Utilize Customer Relationship Management (CRM) software to keep track of your interactions with industry leaders. Tools like Salesforce and HubSpot can help you manage your connections, schedule follow-ups, and ensure that your outreach is timely and organized.

Engaging in Professional Communities and Associations

Joining professional communities and associations can provide structured opportunities to connect with industry leaders who are often active participants in these organizations.

- **Professional Associations**: Become an active member of professional associations relevant to your industry. Attend their events, participate in committees, and contribute to their publications. These activities can increase your visibility and credibility among industry leaders.

- **Online Communities**: Participate in online forums and communities such as Reddit's professional subreddits, Quora, and industry-specific discussion boards. Provide valuable input and establish yourself as a knowledgeable and helpful member. Over time, this can lead to interactions with industry leaders who frequent these platforms.

Offering Value and Building Reciprocity

Industry leaders are often approached by many individuals seeking their attention and advice.

Standing out involves offering something of value in return.

- **Providing Insights**: Share relevant research, data, or insights that can be beneficial to the industry leader's work. This could be a market analysis, a case study, or a novel idea that aligns with their interests.

- **Collaborative Projects**: Propose collaborations on projects, research, or events that align with both your interests and theirs. Working together on a shared initiative can build a strong professional bond.

- **Mentorship and Reverse Mentorship**: Offer your skills and knowledge in areas where the industry leader might benefit. Reverse mentorship, where you provide insights into new technologies or trends, can be particularly valuable.

Following Up and Maintaining Relationships

Building a connection is just the first step; maintaining and nurturing that relationship over time is crucial.

- **Consistent Communication**: Regularly check in with your connections through emails, social media, or professional gatherings. Share updates on your projects and inquire about their work.

- **Personalized Interactions**: Tailor your communications to reflect the unique aspects of your relationship. Reference past conversations, shared interests, and mutual goals.

- **Expressing Gratitude**: Always thank industry leaders for their time and insights. A simple gesture of appreciation can go a long way in maintaining a positive relationship.

By employing these innovative approaches, you can effectively connect with industry leaders, building relationships that are not only beneficial for your career but also enriching for your professional journey. These strategies require effort, creativity, and persistence, but the rewards of establishing connections with influential figures in your field are well worth the investment. Let these methods guide you as you expand your network, ensuring each interaction brings you closer to your professional aspirations.

Chapter 9: Networking Success Stories

Case Studies from Various Industries

Exploring real-world examples of successful networking across different industries provides valuable insights into the diverse ways networking can propel careers and businesses forward. These case studies highlight the strategies, challenges, and outcomes experienced by professionals who have mastered the art of networking, offering actionable lessons for anyone looking to enhance their own networking efforts.

Case Study 1: Technology Industry – The Power of Mentorship Networks

John, a software engineer at a mid-sized tech company, wanted to transition into a leadership role but lacked the necessary management experience. Recognizing the value of mentorship, he strategically connected with senior leaders within his company and the broader tech community.

- **Strategy and Implementation**: John joined industry-specific forums, attended tech meetups, and participated in online webinars where industry leaders were active. He leveraged LinkedIn to reach out to potential mentors, crafting personalized messages that highlighted his goals and how their guidance could be beneficial. His approach was always respectful and showed a genuine interest in learning.

- **Outcome**: Over time, John built a strong network of mentors who provided invaluable advice on leadership, project management, and career growth. Through these connections, he not only gained insights but also received recommendations for leadership development programs. Eventually, this mentorship network helped him secure a managerial position within his company, demonstrating the profound impact of a well-nurtured mentorship network.

Case Study 2: Healthcare Industry – Leveraging Professional Associations

Dr. Sarah, an aspiring pediatrician, understood that building a robust professional network was crucial for her career advancement. She decided to join several professional healthcare associations to expand her network and increase her visibility within the medical community.

- **Strategy and Implementation**: Dr. Sarah actively participated in conferences and workshops hosted by these associations. She volunteered for committees, contributed to association newsletters, and engaged in discussions during events. By being an active member, she positioned herself as a dedicated and knowledgeable professional.

- **Outcome**: Through her involvement in professional associations, Dr. Sarah connected with influential figures in pediatrics, leading to collaborative research opportunities and invitations to speak at conferences. These connections significantly boosted her professional reputation, resulting in a prestigious fellowship and a prominent role in a major pediatric research initiative.

Case Study 3: Finance Industry – Utilizing Social Media for Thought Leadership

Michael, a financial analyst, aimed to establish himself as a thought leader in the finance industry. He recognized that social media could be a powerful tool for building his professional brand and connecting with industry leaders.

- **Strategy and Implementation**: Michael started by creating high-quality content on LinkedIn, focusing on market analysis, investment strategies, and financial trends. He consistently posted articles, shared insights, and engaged with content from other finance professionals. Additionally, he joined LinkedIn groups relevant to his field and participated in discussions to showcase his expertise.

- **Outcome**: Michael's efforts paid off as his content began to attract significant attention. He gained a substantial following on LinkedIn, and his posts were frequently shared and commented on by industry leaders. This visibility led to speaking engagements at financial conferences, invitations to participate in expert panels, and ultimately a promotion to a senior analyst position at his firm. His experience underscores the importance of leveraging social media to build a professional brand and network.

Case Study 4: Education Sector – Building Collaborative Partnerships

Emily, an educational consultant, sought to expand her influence and client base by forming strategic partnerships with other professionals in the education sector. She aimed to create a network that could offer comprehensive educational solutions to schools and institutions.

- **Strategy and Implementation**: Emily attended educational conferences, workshops, and seminars where she could meet other consultants, educators, and administrators. She actively sought out potential partners whose expertise complemented her own. Emily proposed collaborative projects that highlighted mutual benefits, such as co-hosted webinars and joint research initiatives.

- **Outcome**: These partnerships allowed Emily to offer a broader range of services, enhancing her value proposition to clients. Her collaborative approach led to a significant increase in her client base and revenue. Additionally, the partnerships facilitated knowledge exchange and professional growth, positioning her as a leader in the educational consulting field.

Case Study 5: Marketing and Advertising – Engaging Through Innovative Platforms

Lisa, a marketing manager at a leading advertising agency, wanted to connect with top industry executives to explore innovative marketing techniques and trends. She decided to leverage new and emerging platforms to achieve her goal.

- **Strategy and Implementation**: Lisa became an early adopter of Clubhouse, an audio-based social networking app. She joined rooms where marketing and advertising professionals discussed the latest trends and strategies. By actively participating in these discussions and hosting her own rooms on niche marketing topics, she was able to engage directly with industry leaders.

- **Outcome**: Lisa's innovative approach paid off as she formed connections with high-profile executives and influencers in the marketing world. These interactions led to collaborative projects and invitations to exclusive industry events. Her active presence on Clubhouse also enhanced her agency's reputation for being at the forefront of marketing innovation.

Key Takeaways from the Case Studies

- **Mentorship**: Seeking and maintaining relationships with mentors can provide invaluable guidance and open doors to new opportunities.

- **Professional Associations**: Active participation in professional associations can significantly boost visibility and credibility within an industry.

- **Thought Leadership**: Consistently sharing high-quality content on social media can establish you as a thought leader and attract influential connections.

- **Collaborative Partnerships**: Forming strategic partnerships can enhance service offerings and expand professional influence.

- **Innovative Platforms**: Embracing new platforms and technologies can create unique opportunities to connect with industry leaders.

These case studies illustrate that while the specific strategies may vary across industries, the underlying principles of effective networking remain consistent. They highlight the importance of proactive engagement, adding value, and leveraging diverse platforms to build and sustain meaningful professional relationships. By applying these lessons to your own networking efforts, you can navigate the professional landscape with greater confidence and achieve significant career growth.

Analysis of Successful Networking Strategies

Successful networking is a blend of art and science, requiring a strategic approach that combines interpersonal skills, technological savvy, and a deep understanding of social dynamics. By analyzing successful networking strategies across various contexts, we can distill key principles and practices that have proven effective in building and maintaining robust professional relationships.

Strategic Planning and Goal Setting

Effective networking begins with a clear understanding of what you aim to achieve. Setting specific, measurable, achievable, relevant, and time-bound (SMART) goals provides direction and focus for your networking efforts.

- **Example**: Consider a marketing professional aiming to transition into a digital marketing role. Their SMART goals might include attending three industry conferences over the next six months, connecting with ten digital marketing experts on LinkedIn, and securing two informational interviews with industry leaders within the next quarter.

Targeted Outreach

Identifying and reaching out to the right people is critical. Successful networkers often use targeted outreach to connect with individuals who can provide specific insights, opportunities, or introductions.

- **Example**: An aspiring entrepreneur might target successful startup founders and venture capitalists. They could use platforms like LinkedIn to research potential contacts, sending personalized connection requests that reference shared interests or mutual connections to increase the likelihood of a positive response.

Leveraging Existing Connections

Effective networkers understand the value of leveraging existing connections to facilitate new introductions. This approach not only broadens their network but also builds on the trust and credibility already established within their circle.

- **Example**: A project manager seeking to expand their network in the tech industry might ask a current mentor or colleague to introduce them to key players at an upcoming industry event. These introductions often carry more weight and lead to more meaningful connections than cold outreach.

Providing Value First

One of the hallmarks of successful networking is the focus on giving rather than just receiving. Providing value—whether through sharing knowledge, offering assistance, or making introductions—can establish a foundation of goodwill that encourages reciprocity.

- **Example**: A financial analyst might share valuable market insights or offer to review a colleague's investment proposal, demonstrating their expertise and willingness to help. This gesture not only strengthens the relationship but also positions them as a valuable resource.

Consistent Follow-Up

Networking is not a one-time activity but an ongoing process. Consistent follow-up is essential for maintaining and nurturing relationships over time.

- **Example**: After meeting new contacts at a conference, a diligent networker might send personalized follow-up emails within 24-48 hours, referencing specific points from their conversation. They might also schedule regular check-ins, such as quarterly catch-up calls or periodic updates on relevant industry news.

Utilizing Technology and Social Media

In the digital age, technology plays a crucial role in facilitating networking. Successful networkers leverage social media and professional networking platforms to build and maintain their connections.

- **Example**: An HR professional might use LinkedIn to participate in relevant group discussions, share insightful articles, and engage with posts from industry leaders. Tools like CRM software can help track interactions, set reminders for follow-ups, and organize contact information efficiently.

Engaging in Professional Communities

Being actively involved in professional communities, both online and offline, can significantly enhance networking efforts. These communities offer a platform for learning, sharing, and connecting with like-minded individuals.

- **Example**: A software developer might join a local tech meetup group, attend hackathons, and participate in online coding forums. These engagements not only help in building connections but also in staying updated with the latest industry trends and technologies.

Showcasing Thought Leadership

Establishing oneself as a thought leader can attract a wide network of professionals seeking insights and guidance. This can be achieved through content creation, public speaking, and participation in industry events.

- **Example**: A healthcare consultant might write articles for industry publications, speak at conferences, and host webinars on emerging healthcare trends. By sharing their expertise, they build a reputation that attracts connections from across the industry.

Case Studies and Real-World Examples

Analyzing real-world examples of successful networking can provide practical insights and inspiration. For instance, consider how LinkedIn co-founder Reid Hoffman utilized his network to launch and grow LinkedIn. By leveraging his extensive connections in the tech industry, he was able to secure initial funding, attract early adopters, and build a robust platform that revolutionized professional networking.

Adaptability and Resilience

Finally, successful networkers are adaptable and resilient. They are open to new opportunities, willing to pivot their strategies as needed, and persistent in the face of setbacks.

- **Example**: An environmental scientist might face rejections when reaching out to policymakers. Instead of giving up, they could adapt by seeking introductions through mutual contacts or presenting their research in a different format that resonates more with their audience.

Conclusion

Analyzing successful networking strategies reveals that effective networking is a dynamic, multifaceted process that requires strategic planning, targeted outreach, and a focus on providing value. By leveraging technology, engaging in professional communities, and showcasing thought leadership, professionals can build and maintain meaningful connections that drive career growth and success. These principles, when applied consistently and thoughtfully, can transform your networking efforts and open doors to new opportunities and collaborations. Let these insights guide your networking strategy, ensuring each connection contributes to a rich and supportive professional network.

Chapter 10: Your Personal Networking Plan

Crafting a Customized Networking Strategy

Creating a customized networking strategy is essential for achieving specific career goals and maximizing the benefits of your professional connections. A well-tailored approach takes into account your unique strengths, industry dynamics, and personal career objectives, allowing you to build meaningful and effective relationships. Here's a detailed guide on how to craft a customized networking strategy that aligns with your professional aspirations.

Assessing Your Networking Needs and Goals

The first step in developing a personalized networking strategy is to clearly define your objectives. Consider what you want to achieve through networking—whether it's finding a new job, advancing in your current role, gaining industry insights, or expanding your professional influence.

- **Set SMART Goals**: Define Specific, Measurable, Achievable, Relevant, and Time-bound goals. For instance, if you aim to transition into a leadership role within the next year, your networking goals might include attending four industry conferences, connecting with twenty new professionals in leadership positions, and securing mentorship from two senior leaders.

- **Identify Key Outcomes**: Determine the specific outcomes you seek from your networking efforts, such as job referrals, partnerships, mentorship, or knowledge exchange. These outcomes will guide your approach and interactions.

Mapping Your Existing Network

Understanding your current network is crucial for identifying gaps and opportunities. Conduct a thorough inventory of your existing connections to see who might help you reach your goals and where you need to expand.

- **Categorize Contacts**: Group your contacts into categories such as mentors, peers, industry leaders, potential clients, and professional associations. This helps you see the diversity and depth of your network.

- **Assess Connection Strength**: Evaluate the strength and quality of each connection.

Consider how often you communicate, the nature of your interactions, and the mutual value of the relationship.

Identifying Target Contacts

Once you understand your existing network, identify the new connections you need to make to achieve your goals. Focus on individuals who can provide unique insights, opportunities, or introductions.

- **Industry Leaders and Influencers**: Connect with thought leaders and influencers in your field. These individuals can offer valuable guidance and open doors to new opportunities.

- **Peers and Colleagues**: Don't overlook the value of peer connections. Your peers can provide support, share knowledge, and collaborate on projects.

- **Professional Organizations**: Join and actively participate in professional associations relevant to your industry. These organizations offer numerous networking opportunities and resources.

Utilizing Multiple Networking Channels

To build a robust network, leverage various channels and platforms. Each channel offers different advantages and can help you connect with a diverse range of professionals.

- **Online Platforms**: Use LinkedIn, Twitter, and industry-specific forums to engage with professionals globally. Participate in discussions, share valuable content, and connect with key individuals.

- **Industry Events**: Attend conferences, seminars, and workshops to meet professionals in person. Prepare in advance by researching attendees and planning who you want to meet.

- **Webinars and Virtual Events**: Participate in online events to connect with professionals remotely. These platforms often provide opportunities for interaction and networking through chat features and breakout rooms.

- **Alumni Networks**: Reconnect with alumni from your alma mater. Alumni networks are often supportive and can provide valuable introductions and opportunities.

Building and Maintaining Relationships

Establishing connections is only the beginning. To reap the full benefits of networking, you must cultivate and maintain these relationships over time.

- **Regular Communication**: Keep in touch with your contacts through regular updates, check-ins, and follow-ups. Share industry news, congratulate them on achievements, and show genuine interest in their progress.
- **Add Value**: Continuously seek ways to provide value to your connections. Share resources, offer assistance, and make introductions that could benefit them.
- **Personalization**: Tailor your interactions based on each contact's interests and needs. Personalized communication demonstrates your commitment and respect for the relationship.

Evaluating and Adjusting Your Strategy

Networking is an ongoing process that requires regular evaluation and adjustment. Periodically review your strategy to ensure it remains aligned with your goals and industry trends.

- **Track Progress**: Monitor your progress towards your networking goals. Keep a record of new connections, interactions, and outcomes.

- **Solicit Feedback**: Seek feedback from your network on your approach and interactions. This can provide valuable insights for improvement.

- **Adjust Goals and Tactics**: As you achieve certain milestones or as your career goals evolve, adjust your networking goals and tactics accordingly. Stay flexible and open to new opportunities.

Leveraging Technology and Tools

Utilize technology to streamline your networking efforts and maintain organization. Tools such as CRM software, LinkedIn's premium features, and networking apps can enhance your efficiency and effectiveness.

- **CRM Software**: Use tools like HubSpot or Salesforce to manage your contacts, track interactions, and schedule follow-ups.

- **LinkedIn Premium**: Take advantage of LinkedIn's advanced features for expanded search capabilities, InMail messaging, and detailed profile insights.

- **Networking Apps**: Explore apps like Shapr and Bumble Bizz for additional networking opportunities and connections.

Conclusion

Crafting a customized networking strategy involves a thoughtful and strategic approach tailored to your unique career goals and strengths. By setting clear objectives, mapping your existing network, identifying target contacts, utilizing multiple channels, and maintaining relationships, you can build a powerful network that supports your professional growth. Regular evaluation and adjustment ensure that your strategy remains effective and relevant. Embrace this comprehensive approach to networking, and watch as it transforms your career, opening doors to new opportunities and collaborations.

Tools and Resources to Get Started

Embarking on a journey to master the art of networking requires more than just motivation; it necessitates the right tools and resources to effectively build and manage your professional relationships. With a plethora of options available, it's crucial to identify those that align with your networking goals and industry needs. This comprehensive guide will walk you through the essential tools and resources you need to get started and succeed in your networking endeavors.

Professional Networking Platforms

Professional networking platforms are the cornerstone of modern networking efforts. These platforms provide the infrastructure to connect with industry peers, leaders, and potential mentors.

- **LinkedIn**: The premier platform for professional networking, LinkedIn allows you to create a detailed profile, connect with professionals globally, join industry-specific groups, and share content to establish thought leadership. Utilize LinkedIn's advanced search functions to find and connect with key individuals, and take advantage of its premium features for enhanced networking capabilities.

- **Xing**: Popular in Europe, Xing is another valuable platform for building professional connections. It offers similar features to LinkedIn, including profile creation, networking groups, and event listings.

Customer Relationship Management (CRM) Software

CRM software helps manage and maintain relationships by organizing contacts, tracking interactions, and scheduling follow-ups. These tools ensure that no connection falls through the cracks.

- **HubSpot CRM**: HubSpot offers a robust free CRM tool that helps you track your communications and manage your professional relationships efficiently. It integrates with your email, calendar, and social media accounts to provide a seamless networking experience.

- **Salesforce**: While primarily used for sales, Salesforce's CRM capabilities are highly effective for networking. It allows for detailed contact management, task automation, and analytics to monitor your networking efforts.

Email Marketing Tools

Regular communication is key to maintaining relationships. Email marketing tools allow you to send personalized messages, newsletters, and updates to your network.

- **Mailchimp**: Mailchimp is a user-friendly email marketing tool that allows you to create and send newsletters, automate follow-up emails, and segment your audience for targeted communication.

- **Constant Contact**: This platform offers similar features to Mailchimp, with additional tools for managing events and surveys, making it ideal for comprehensive network management.

Social Media Management Tools

Managing your presence across multiple social media platforms can be daunting. Social media management tools help you schedule posts, monitor interactions, and analyze your social media performance.

- **Hootsuite**: Hootsuite allows you to manage multiple social media accounts from a single dashboard. Schedule posts, track engagement, and analyze performance to optimize your social media networking efforts.

- **Buffer**: Buffer offers similar functionality with a focus on simplicity and ease of use. It's ideal for scheduling posts and tracking basic analytics across various social media platforms.

Event Management Platforms

Attending and hosting events are crucial aspects of networking. Event management platforms help you find relevant events, manage registrations, and facilitate virtual networking.

- **Eventbrite**: Eventbrite is a popular platform for discovering and registering for professional events. It also allows you to host your own events, manage attendees, and promote your events to a broader audience.

- **Meetup**: Meetup focuses on bringing people together in person or virtually around shared interests. It's an excellent tool for finding local networking events and professional groups.

Content Creation and Sharing Tools

Establishing yourself as a thought leader in your industry involves creating and sharing valuable content. Content creation tools help you produce high-quality articles, videos, and graphics.

- **Canva**: Canva is an intuitive design tool that allows you to create professional-looking graphics, presentations, and social media posts. It's perfect for creating visually appealing content to share with your network.

- **Medium**: Medium is a blogging platform that allows you to publish long-form articles and reach a broad audience. It's an excellent way to share your expertise and engage with industry peers.

Virtual Meeting and Collaboration Tools

In today's digital age, virtual meetings have become an essential part of networking. These tools facilitate remote communication and collaboration.

- **Zoom**: Zoom is a leading video conferencing tool that offers high-quality video and audio, screen sharing, and recording features. It's ideal for virtual networking events, webinars, and one-on-one meetings.
- **Microsoft Teams**: Teams integrates with Microsoft Office and provides robust features for virtual meetings, chat, and collaboration. It's particularly useful for networking within organizations or industry groups.

Professional Development Resources

Continual learning and professional development are vital for effective networking. Leverage online courses, webinars, and industry publications to stay informed and improve your skills.

- **Coursera**: Coursera offers online courses from top universities and companies. Enroll in courses on networking, communication, and industry-specific skills to enhance your knowledge and credibility.

- **Harvard Business Review**: Subscribe to industry-leading publications like the Harvard Business Review for insights into business trends, leadership strategies, and networking tips.

Books and Podcasts

Books and podcasts provide in-depth knowledge and inspiration. They offer practical advice, success stories, and strategies from experts in the field.

- **Books**: "Never Eat Alone" by Keith Ferrazzi, "How to Win Friends and Influence People" by Dale Carnegie, and "The Tipping Point" by Malcolm Gladwell are must-reads for networking enthusiasts.

- **Podcasts**: Listen to podcasts like "The Tim Ferriss Show," "How I Built This," and "The Jordan Harbinger Show" for interviews with successful networkers and entrepreneurs.

Conclusion

Equipping yourself with the right tools and resources is the foundation of effective networking. By leveraging professional networking platforms, CRM software, email marketing tools, and social media management tools, you can streamline your networking efforts and maintain meaningful connections. Additionally, attending events, creating valuable content, utilizing virtual meeting tools, and engaging in continual professional development will enhance your ability to build and sustain a robust professional network. These resources, when used strategically, will empower you to achieve your networking goals and advance your career. Dive into these tools and resources, integrate them into your networking strategy, and watch your professional relationships flourish.

Conclusion

Recap of Key Points

As we reach the culmination of "Connective Career Crafting: Mastering the Art of Networking and Relationship Building for Professional Success," it is essential to revisit and encapsulate the fundamental principles and strategies that have been covered. This comprehensive review aims to reinforce the key insights and actionable steps that will empower you to excel in your networking endeavors and achieve sustained professional growth.

The Foundations of Networking

We began by establishing a clear definition of professional networking and exploring its historical context and evolution. Networking is not merely about exchanging business cards or adding connections on social media; it is about building meaningful relationships that can provide mutual support and opportunities. We traced the origins of networking, from early trade guilds to modern digital platforms, highlighting how the core principles have remained consistent even as the tools and methods have evolved.

Mapping and Assessing Your Network

Understanding your existing network is a crucial step in effective networking. By conducting an inventory of your current connections and assessing the strength of these ties, you can identify gaps and opportunities. We discussed methods to categorize and evaluate your contacts, ensuring that you have a balanced network that includes mentors, peers, and industry leaders. This assessment allows you to develop a strategic plan to enhance and expand your network.

The Psychology Behind Effective Networking

Effective networking is deeply rooted in understanding social dynamics and human behavior. Building rapport and trust are foundational elements that can make or break your networking efforts. We delved into the psychological aspects of networking, such as the importance of active listening, empathy, and emotional intelligence. These skills enable you to connect with others on a deeper level, fostering genuine and long-lasting relationships.

Strategic Networking for Career Growth

Networking with purpose is essential for career advancement. We explored various strategies for strategic networking at conferences, events, and through social media platforms. Whether attending industry conferences or engaging in online discussions, the key is to be intentional and proactive. We provided practical tips on how to prepare for networking events, initiate conversations, and follow up effectively to maintain the connections you make.

Mastering Communication Skills

Communication is at the heart of networking. We emphasized the importance of both verbal and non-verbal communication skills, including the nuances of body language, tone of voice, and the power of active listening. By honing these skills, you can present yourself more effectively, convey your ideas clearly, and understand others better, making your interactions more impactful.

Building and Maintaining Diverse Relationships

A diverse network is a strong network. We discussed the benefits of cultivating relationships across different industries, backgrounds, and levels of experience. This diversity not only broadens your perspective but also provides access to a wider range of opportunities and resources. Long-term relationship management involves consistent and thoughtful communication, providing value, and being reliable and trustworthy.

Overcoming Networking Challenges

Networking is not without its challenges. We identified common pitfalls such as fear of rejection, lack of confidence, and difficulty in maintaining relationships. Strategies to overcome these obstacles include developing a growth mindset, practicing resilience, and learning from setbacks. We also addressed how to deal with rejection and use it as a learning opportunity to improve your networking approach.

Advanced Networking Techniques

In today's digital age, leveraging technology is indispensable. We covered advanced techniques such as using CRM tools to manage contacts, engaging on professional networking platforms like LinkedIn, and utilizing innovative approaches like virtual events and webinars. These tools and techniques can significantly enhance your ability to connect with and stay engaged with your network.

Learning from Success Stories

Real-world case studies from various industries illustrated the practical application of networking strategies. These success stories provided concrete examples of how individuals have effectively used networking to achieve their career goals. Analyzing these stories helped to highlight best practices and inspire actionable insights that you can apply to your own networking efforts.

Creating Your Personal Networking Plan

Finally, we guided you through crafting a customized networking strategy tailored to your specific career objectives and strengths. This involved setting SMART goals, identifying target contacts, and utilizing a mix of networking channels to build a robust and dynamic network. A personalized plan ensures that your networking efforts are focused, efficient, and aligned with your career aspirations.

Conclusion

By now, you should have a comprehensive understanding of the principles and practices that underpin successful networking. The strategies and insights provided in this book are designed to empower you to build and maintain a network that supports your professional growth and opens up new opportunities. Networking is a dynamic, ongoing process that requires commitment, adaptability, and a genuine interest in connecting with others.

As you continue to refine your networking skills and expand your professional relationships, remember that the key to success lies in authenticity, consistency, and the willingness to provide value to others. Embrace the journey of networking with confidence and enthusiasm, and watch as it transforms your career and enriches your professional life.

Encouragement for Continuous Networking Effort

Embarking on a networking journey is a significant step toward achieving professional success, but the key to long-term benefits lies in continuous effort and sustained engagement. Networking is not a one-time event but an ongoing process that evolves with your career. To truly harness the power of your professional relationships, it is essential to maintain a consistent and proactive approach. This section aims to inspire and motivate you to keep nurturing and expanding your network, ensuring that it remains a vital asset throughout your professional life.

Embrace the Journey

Networking is a marathon, not a sprint. It requires patience, persistence, and a genuine interest in building and maintaining relationships. Each interaction, whether at a conference, on social media, or through a casual conversation, contributes to the broader tapestry of your professional network. Embrace the journey with an open mind and a positive attitude. Celebrate small victories, such as reconnecting with an old colleague or making a new contact, as these incremental steps collectively lead to significant career advancements.

Set Regular Networking Goals

To stay motivated, set regular and achievable networking goals. These goals can be as simple as attending one industry event per month, reaching out to two new contacts each week, or scheduling a quarterly catch-up with your mentors. By breaking down your networking efforts into manageable tasks, you can maintain momentum and avoid feeling overwhelmed. Regularly review and adjust your goals to align with your evolving career objectives and interests.

Leverage Technology for Consistency

In the digital age, numerous tools and platforms can help you stay organized and consistent in your networking efforts. Utilize customer relationship management (CRM) software to track your interactions, schedule follow-ups, and set reminders for important networking activities. Social media platforms like LinkedIn offer features that help you stay updated with your connections' career milestones, enabling you to engage meaningfully and timely. Consistency in your networking efforts builds reliability and trust, which are crucial for maintaining strong professional relationships.

Continual Learning and Adaptation

The landscape of networking is constantly changing, driven by technological advancements and shifting industry trends. To stay ahead, commit to continual learning and adaptation. Attend webinars, read industry publications, and participate in professional development courses to keep your skills and knowledge current. Adapt your networking strategies to leverage new tools and platforms that emerge, ensuring that your approach remains relevant and effective.

Give Before You Receive

A fundamental principle of effective networking is the concept of giving before you receive. Offer assistance, share resources, and provide value to your network without expecting immediate returns. This generosity fosters goodwill and strengthens your relationships. When you consistently offer support and value, your contacts are more likely to reciprocate, creating a mutually beneficial dynamic. This approach not only enhances your reputation but also builds a network rooted in trust and collaboration.

Resilience in the Face of Setbacks

Networking, like any other aspect of professional life, can come with its share of setbacks and rejections. It's important to approach these challenges with resilience and a growth mindset. Instead of being discouraged by a lack of immediate results or a rejection, view these experiences as learning opportunities. Reflect on what you can improve and adjust your strategies accordingly. Resilience will keep you moving forward, even when faced with obstacles, and ultimately lead to more robust and fruitful connections.

Celebrate and Reflect on Achievements

Take time to celebrate your networking achievements and reflect on your progress. Acknowledge the milestones you've reached, such as forming a key connection, receiving valuable advice, or gaining a new opportunity through your network. Reflecting on these successes can boost your motivation and provide insight into what strategies are working well. Use these reflections to refine your approach and set new, ambitious goals.

Maintain Authenticity and Integrity

Authenticity and integrity are the cornerstones of meaningful networking. Be genuine in your interactions and maintain a high level of professionalism. Authenticity fosters trust and respect, making your connections more likely to engage with you and offer their support. Integrity ensures that your actions are aligned with your values and ethical standards, further solidifying your reputation as a reliable and trustworthy professional.

Expand Beyond Comfort Zones

To maximize the potential of your network, be willing to step outside your comfort zones. Attend events in different industries, connect with professionals from diverse backgrounds, and explore new areas of interest. Expanding your network beyond your immediate field can provide fresh perspectives, innovative ideas, and unexpected opportunities. Diversity in your network enriches your professional life and broadens your horizons.

In Conclusion

Continuous networking effort is essential for sustained professional growth and success. By embracing the journey, setting regular goals, leveraging technology, continually learning, giving generously, showing resilience, celebrating achievements, maintaining authenticity, and expanding beyond comfort zones, you can build and sustain a powerful professional network. This network will not only support your current career aspirations but also open doors to new opportunities and collaborations in the future. Keep the momentum going, stay proactive, and watch as your network transforms your career in profound and meaningful ways.

Appendices

Templates for Networking Outreach

Effective networking often begins with a well-crafted initial outreach. Whether you're reconnecting with an old contact, reaching out to a new one, or following up after a meeting, the right template can make all the difference. In this section, we will explore detailed templates for various networking scenarios. These templates are designed to help you convey professionalism, sincerity, and value, making your networking efforts more efficient and impactful.

Reaching Out to a New Contact

When contacting someone for the first time, it's crucial to be clear, concise, and respectful of their time. Personalize your message to show genuine interest and relevance.

Subject: Exploring Opportunities for Collaboration

Dear [Name],

I hope this message finds you well. My name is [Your Name], and I am currently [Your Position] at

[Your Company/Organization]. I recently came across your profile and was particularly impressed by your work in [Specific Area/Project/Industry].

I am reaching out to explore potential opportunities for collaboration between us. With your expertise in [Field/Industry], I believe there are several ways we could benefit from each other's insights and experiences. Specifically, I am interested in discussing [Briefly Mention Your Interest or Proposal].

Would you be available for a brief call or meeting next week to discuss this further? I am flexible with my schedule and can adjust to a time that works best for you.

Thank you for considering this opportunity. I look forward to the possibility of connecting with you.

Best regards,
[Your Name]
[Your Contact Information]
[LinkedIn Profile or Other Relevant Link]

Following Up After a Networking Event

Following up after meeting someone at a conference or event is essential to keep the connection alive. Reference your previous interaction to remind them of your conversation.

Subject: Great Meeting You at [Event Name]!

Hi [Name],

I hope you're doing well. It was a pleasure meeting you at [Event Name] last [Day/Date]. I truly enjoyed our conversation about [Specific Topic You Discussed].

As we discussed, I would love to continue our conversation and explore potential ways we could collaborate or support each other. Your insights into [Specific Area] were particularly valuable, and I believe there are opportunities for us to leverage our respective strengths.

Would you be open to setting up a call or coffee meeting sometime next week? I am keen to hear more about your work with [Their Company/Project] and discuss how we might work together.

Looking forward to reconnecting soon.

Best,
[Your Name]
[Your Contact Information]
[LinkedIn Profile or Other Relevant Link]

Reconnecting with an Old Contact

Reconnecting with someone you haven't spoken to in a while requires a balance of courtesy and a reminder of your past relationship.

Subject: Long Time, No See – Let's Catch Up!

Hello [Name],

I hope this message finds you well. It's been a while since we last connected, and I thought it would be a good time to catch up. I recently came across [Their Work/Article/Post] and was reminded of our great conversations about [Topic/Shared Interest].

Since we last spoke, I've been [Briefly Share What You've Been Up To]. I would love to hear about what you've been working on and how things are going for you at [Their Company/Current Endeavor].

Would you be interested in catching up over a call or coffee sometime soon? It would be great to reconnect and exchange updates.

Warm regards,
[Your Name]
[Your Contact Information]
[LinkedIn Profile or Other Relevant Link]

Requesting an Informational Interview

When seeking advice or insights from someone in your industry, it's important to be respectful of their time and clearly state your intentions.

Subject: Seeking Your Advice on [Specific Topic/Industry]

Dear [Name],

I hope this message finds you well. My name is [Your Name], and I am currently [Your Position/Role] at [Your Company/Organization]. I have been following your work in [Specific Field/Industry] for some time and greatly admire your achievements and contributions.

I am reaching out to request an informational interview to gain insights into [Specific Topic/Area]. As someone with extensive experience in [Their Industry/Field], your perspective would be incredibly valuable to me.

Would you be available for a 20-30 minute call at your convenience? I am flexible and can adjust to a time that works best for you.

Thank you very much for considering my request. I appreciate your time and look forward to the opportunity to learn from your experiences.

Sincerely,
[Your Name]
[Your Contact Information]
[LinkedIn Profile or Other Relevant Link]

Thanking Someone for Their Help or Advice

Expressing gratitude for someone's assistance not only acknowledges their support but also strengthens the relationship.

Subject: Thank You for Your Guidance

Hi [Name],

I hope you're doing well. I wanted to take a moment to thank you for the valuable advice you provided regarding [Specific Topic/Issue]. Your insights were incredibly helpful, and I have already begun to implement some of your suggestions.

I truly appreciate you taking the time to share your expertise with me. If there's ever anything I can do to return the favor, please don't hesitate to let me know.

Thank you once again for your support.

Best regards,
[Your Name]
[Your Contact Information]
[LinkedIn Profile or Other Relevant Link]

Inviting Someone to a Networking Event

Inviting a contact to an event can be a great way to nurture the relationship and provide value.

Subject: Invitation to [Event Name]

Dear [Name],

I hope this message finds you well. I wanted to personally invite you to [Event Name] on [Date] at [Location]. The event will focus on [Brief Description of the Event] and will feature speakers and discussions on [Specific Topics of Interest].

Given your expertise in [Their Field/Industry], I believe you would find the event both enjoyable and valuable. It would also be a great opportunity to connect with other professionals in our industry.

I would be delighted if you could join me. Please let me know if you're available, and I can share more details.

Looking forward to hearing from you.

Best,
[Your Name]
[Your Contact Information]
[LinkedIn Profile or Other Relevant Link]

Conclusion

Utilizing these templates can streamline your networking efforts and help you craft messages that are both professional and personable. Remember to personalize each template to fit the context and the individual you are reaching out to. Networking is about building genuine relationships, and thoughtful, well-crafted communication is a crucial step in that process. By using these templates as a starting point, you can confidently engage with your network, foster meaningful connections, and advance your professional goals.

Recommended Reading and Resources

To further enhance your networking skills and broaden your understanding of professional relationship building, I have compiled a comprehensive list of recommended readings and resources. These books, articles, podcasts, and online platforms will provide additional insights, practical tips, and inspiration as you continue to develop and refine your networking strategy. Each resource has been selected based on its relevance, authority, and ability to offer unique perspectives on networking and career development.

Books on Networking and Professional Development

1. **"Never Eat Alone: And Other Secrets to Success, One Relationship at a Time" by Keith Ferrazzi**

    - This classic book emphasizes the importance of building meaningful relationships and provides practical advice on how to connect with others effectively. Ferrazzi's personal anecdotes and actionable tips make it a must-read for anyone serious about networking.

2. **"The Lean Startup: How Today's Entrepreneurs Use Continuous Innovation to Create Radically Successful Businesses" by Eric Ries**

    - While primarily focused on entrepreneurship, this book offers valuable lessons on the importance of networking within the startup ecosystem. Ries's insights into building connections that foster innovation are applicable across various industries.

3. **"Give and Take: Why Helping Others Drives Our Success" by Adam Grant**

- Grant explores how different networking styles—givers, takers, and matchers—impact professional success. This book provides a research-backed perspective on the benefits of generosity and reciprocity in networking.

4. **"Dare to Lead: Brave Work. Tough Conversations. Whole Hearts." by Brené Brown**

    - Brown's work on leadership and vulnerability is essential for understanding how to build trust and authentic relationships in a professional context. Her insights into courage and empathy are crucial for effective networking.

5. **"The Tipping Point: How Little Things Can Make a Big Difference" by Malcolm Gladwell**

    - Gladwell's exploration of how small changes can create significant impacts includes valuable lessons on the power of networking. Understanding the dynamics of social networks can help you leverage your connections more effectively.

Articles and Journals

1. **"The Network Secrets of Great Change Agents" by Julie Battilana and Tiziana Casciaro (Harvard Business Review)**
   - This article delves into the characteristics that make some individuals more effective at networking and driving change within organizations. It offers practical advice for enhancing your networking capabilities.

2. **"How to Build Your Network" by Brian Uzzi and Shannon Dunlap (Harvard Business Review)**
   - Uzzi and Dunlap provide a comprehensive guide to developing a robust professional network. Their insights into the structure and dynamics of networks are invaluable for strategic networking.

3. **"Networking Your Way to Success" by Herminia Ibarra (Stanford Social Innovation Review)**
   - Ibarra's article focuses on the importance of networking for career advancement and provides strategies

for building and maintaining professional relationships.

Podcasts

1. **"How I Built This" with Guy Raz**
   - This podcast features interviews with entrepreneurs and innovators, highlighting the networking strategies that contributed to their success. Listening to these stories can provide inspiration and practical tips for your networking efforts.

2. **"The Tim Ferriss Show"**
   - Tim Ferriss interviews top performers across various fields, discussing their routines, habits, and networking strategies. This podcast offers valuable insights into how successful individuals build and leverage their networks.

3. **"Networking and Relationships" by Jordan Harbinger**
   - Harbinger's podcast focuses on building and maintaining professional relationships. His episodes cover a

wide range of topics, from social dynamics to practical networking tips.

Online Platforms and Communities

1. **LinkedIn Learning**
   - LinkedIn Learning offers a variety of courses on networking, communication, and professional development. These courses are designed to provide actionable skills and strategies for enhancing your networking efforts.

2. **Coursera**
   - Coursera provides access to courses from top universities and institutions, covering topics related to networking, leadership, and career development. These courses can help you build a solid foundation in networking principles.

3. **Meetup**
   - Meetup is a platform that allows you to find and join local groups based on your interests and professional goals. Participating in these groups can help

you expand your network and connect with like-minded individuals.

4. **Slack Communities**
    - Many industries have Slack communities where professionals gather to share knowledge, opportunities, and support. Joining these communities can help you stay updated on industry trends and build relationships with peers.

Professional Associations and Networking Groups

1. **Professional Associations**
    - Joining professional associations relevant to your industry can provide access to networking events, resources, and mentorship opportunities. Examples include the American Marketing Association (AMA), the Project Management Institute (PMI), and the Society for Human Resource Management (SHRM).

2. **Networking Groups**
    - Networking groups such as BNI (Business Network International) and

Toastmasters International offer structured environments for developing networking skills and building professional relationships. These groups provide regular opportunities for practice and feedback.

Conclusion

By leveraging these recommended readings and resources, you can deepen your understanding of networking principles and continuously improve your networking skills. The knowledge and strategies gained from these resources will empower you to build and maintain a dynamic, effective professional network that supports your career aspirations. Keep exploring, learning, and applying these insights to transform your networking efforts into meaningful and lasting connections.

Summary

Introduction 3
   The Vital Role of Networking in Today's Job Market 3
   Overview of the Book 6
Chapter 1: The Foundations of Networking 10
   Defining Professional Networking 10
   Historical Perspective and Evolution 13
Chapter 2: Mapping Your Existing Network 17
   Inventory of Current Connections 17
   Assessing the Strength of Your Ties 20
      Methods to Assess the Strength of Your Network 22
      Strategic Application of This Assessment 23
Chapter 3: The Psychology Behind Effective Networking .. 25
   Understanding Social Dynamics in Professional Settings 25
      Strategies to Master Social Dynamics in Professional Settings 27
   Building Rapport and Trust 29
      Strategies for Building Rapport 30
      Strategies for Building Trust 31
Chapter 4: Networking Strategies for Career Growth 34
   Strategic Networking at Conferences and Events 34
      Effective Tactics for Conference Networking 35
      Leveraging Technology and Social Media 36
      Networking with a Purpose 37

Leveraging Social Media and Online Platforms 38

Chapter 5: Mastering the Art of Communication 42

    Verbal and Non-verbal Communication Skills 42

        Practicing Communication Skills 44

    Listening: The Key to Successful Networking 46

        The Importance of Active Listening in Networking 46

        Techniques for Enhancing Listening Skills 47

        Listening in Different Contexts 48

Chapter 6: Building and Maintaining Diverse Professional Relationships 50

    Cultivating a Diverse Network 50

        Why Diversity Matters in Professional Networking 50

        Strategies for Building a Diverse Network 51

        The Impact of a Diverse Network 53

    Long-Term Relationship Management 54

        The Foundations of Sustaining Professional Relationships 54

        Advanced Strategies for Long-Term Relationship Management 56

        Conclusion 57

Chapter 7: Networking Challenges and Solutions 59

    Common Pitfalls and How to Avoid Them 59

        Overlooking Follow-Up 59

        Focusing Too Much on Quantity Over Quality 60

        Neglecting Diverse Connections 60

        Undervaluing Soft Skills 61

  Being Overly Aggressive or Salesy.. 61
  Lack of Preparation.. 62
  Failure to Adapt to Different Cultural Norms................. 62
 Dealing with Rejection and Setbacks.. 63
  Understanding the Nature of Rejection in Networking 64
  Strategies for Overcoming and Learning from Rejection 64
  Long-Term Management of Setbacks 66
Chapter 8: Advanced Networking Techniques........................ 68
 Utilizing Technology for Networking 68
  The Role of Social Media in Professional Networking 68
  Professional Networking Apps 70
  Virtual Events and Webinars 70
  Email and CRM Tools... 71
  Innovative Networking Technologies 72
  Best Practices for Utilizing Technology in Networking 73
 Innovative Approaches to Connect with Industry Leaders 74
  Leveraging Content Creation 74
  Hosting and Attending Webinars... 75
  Utilizing Technology and Tools... 76
  Engaging in Professional Communities and Associations 77
  Offering Value and Building Reciprocity 77
  Following Up and Maintaining Relationships 78

Chapter 9: Networking Success Stories 80

   Case Studies from Various Industries 80

      Case Study 1: Technology Industry – The Power of Mentorship Networks 80

      Case Study 2: Healthcare Industry – Leveraging Professional Associations 81

      Case Study 3: Finance Industry – Utilizing Social Media for Thought Leadership 82

      Case Study 4: Education Sector – Building Collaborative Partnerships 83

      Case Study 5: Marketing and Advertising – Engaging Through Innovative Platforms 84

      Key Takeaways from the Case Studies 85

   Analysis of Successful Networking Strategies 86

      Strategic Planning and Goal Setting 87

      Targeted Outreach 87

      Leveraging Existing Connections 88

      Providing Value First 88

      Consistent Follow-Up 89

      Utilizing Technology and Social Media 89

      Engaging in Professional Communities 90

      Showcasing Thought Leadership 90

      Case Studies and Real-World Examples 91

      Adaptability and Resilience 91

      Conclusion 92

Chapter 10: Your Personal Networking Plan 93

   Crafting a Customized Networking Strategy 93

- Assessing Your Networking Needs and Goals 93
- Mapping Your Existing Network 94
- Identifying Target Contacts 95
- Utilizing Multiple Networking Channels 96
- Building and Maintaining Relationships 97
- Evaluating and Adjusting Your Strategy 97
- Leveraging Technology and Tools 98
- Conclusion 99
- Tools and Resources to Get Started 99
  - Professional Networking Platforms 100
  - Customer Relationship Management (CRM) Software 101
  - Email Marketing Tools 101
  - Social Media Management Tools 102
  - Event Management Platforms 103
  - Content Creation and Sharing Tools 103
  - Virtual Meeting and Collaboration Tools 104
  - Professional Development Resources 104
  - Books and Podcasts 105
  - Conclusion 106
- Conclusion 107
  - Recap of Key Points 107
  - The Foundations of Networking 107
  - Mapping and Assessing Your Network 108
  - The Psychology Behind Effective Networking 108
  - Strategic Networking for Career Growth 108

- Mastering Communication Skills 109
- Building and Maintaining Diverse Relationships 109
- Overcoming Networking Challenges 110
- Advanced Networking Techniques 110
- Learning from Success Stories 110
- Creating Your Personal Networking Plan 111
- Conclusion 111
- Encouragement for Continuous Networking Effort 112
  - Embrace the Journey 112
  - Set Regular Networking Goals 113
  - Leverage Technology for Consistency 113
  - Continual Learning and Adaptation 114
  - Give Before You Receive 114
  - Resilience in the Face of Setbacks 115
  - Celebrate and Reflect on Achievements 115
  - Maintain Authenticity and Integrity 116
  - Expand Beyond Comfort Zones 116
  - In Conclusion 116
- Appendices 118
  - Templates for Networking Outreach 118
    - Reaching Out to a New Contact 118
    - Following Up After a Networking Event 119
    - Reconnecting with an Old Contact 121
    - Requesting an Informational Interview 122
    - Thanking Someone for Their Help or Advice 123
    - Inviting Someone to a Networking Event 124

Conclusion..125
Recommended Reading and Resources 125
    Books on Networking and Professional Development 126
    Articles and Journals 128
    Podcasts 129
    Online Platforms and Communities................................130
    Professional Associations and Networking Groups..131
    Conclusion..132

www.ingramcontent.com/pod-product-compliance
Lightning Source LLC
Chambersburg PA
CBHW050104230526
45470CB00004B/1674